AF248698

The Rockabillies

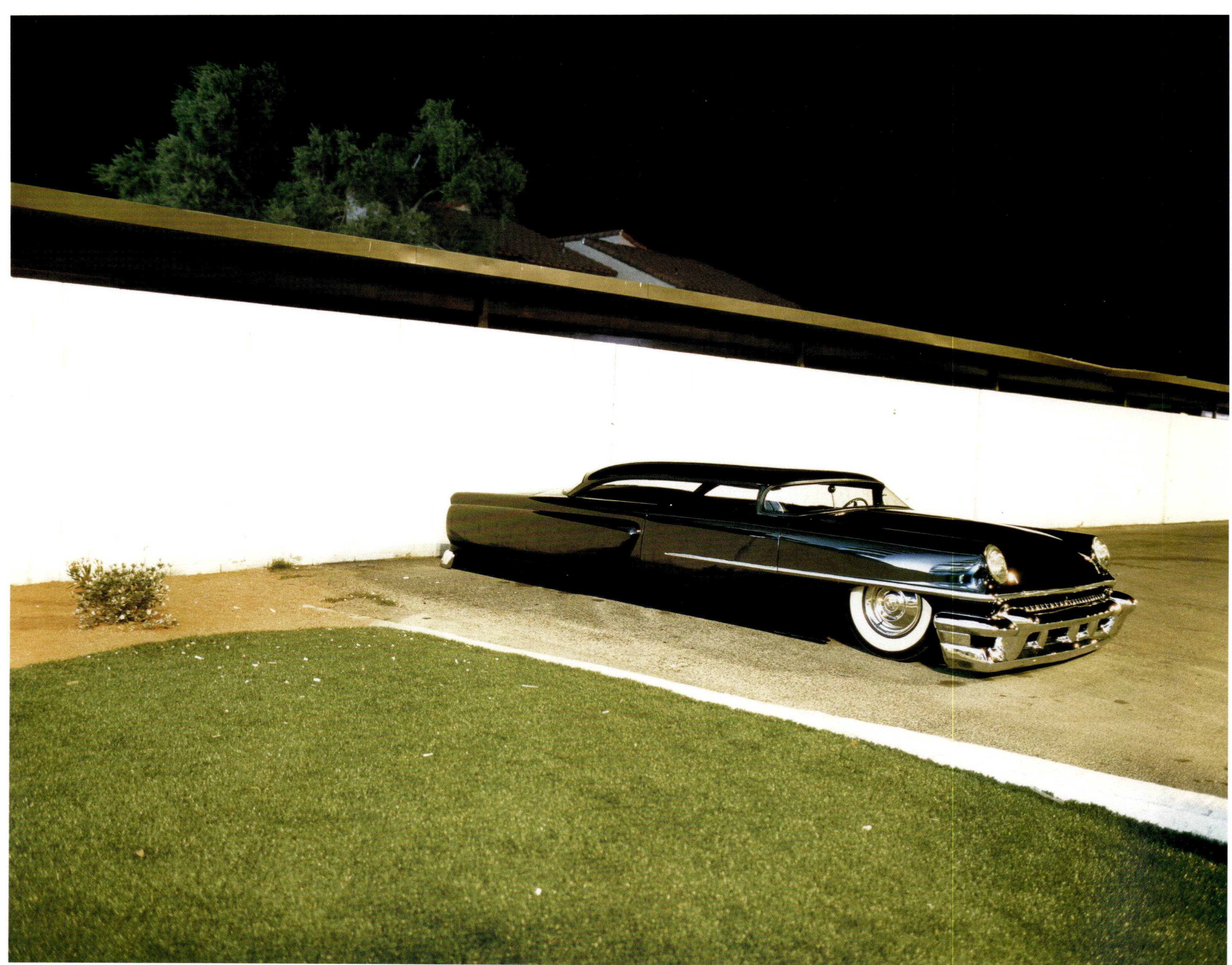

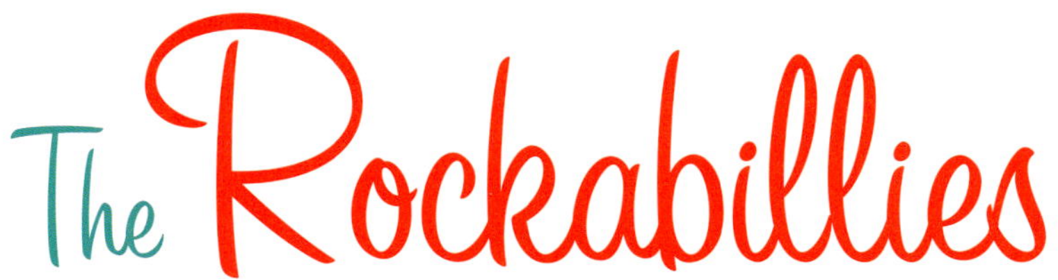The Rockabillies

JENNIFER GREENBURG

with essays by Bruce Berenson and Audrey Michelle Mast

Center Books on American Places
George F. Thompson, series founder and director

The Center for American Places
at Columbia College Chicago

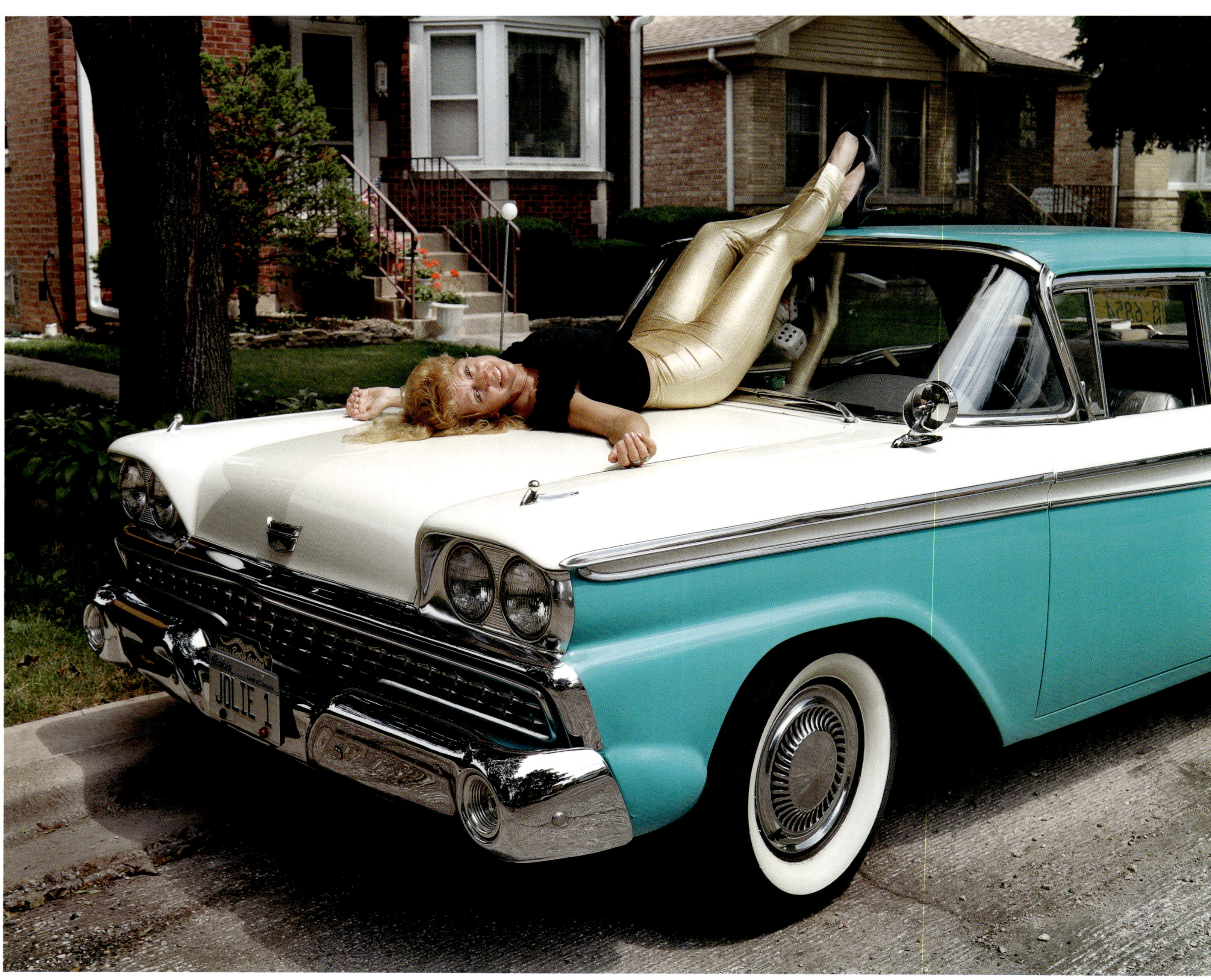

JOLIE 1

Contents

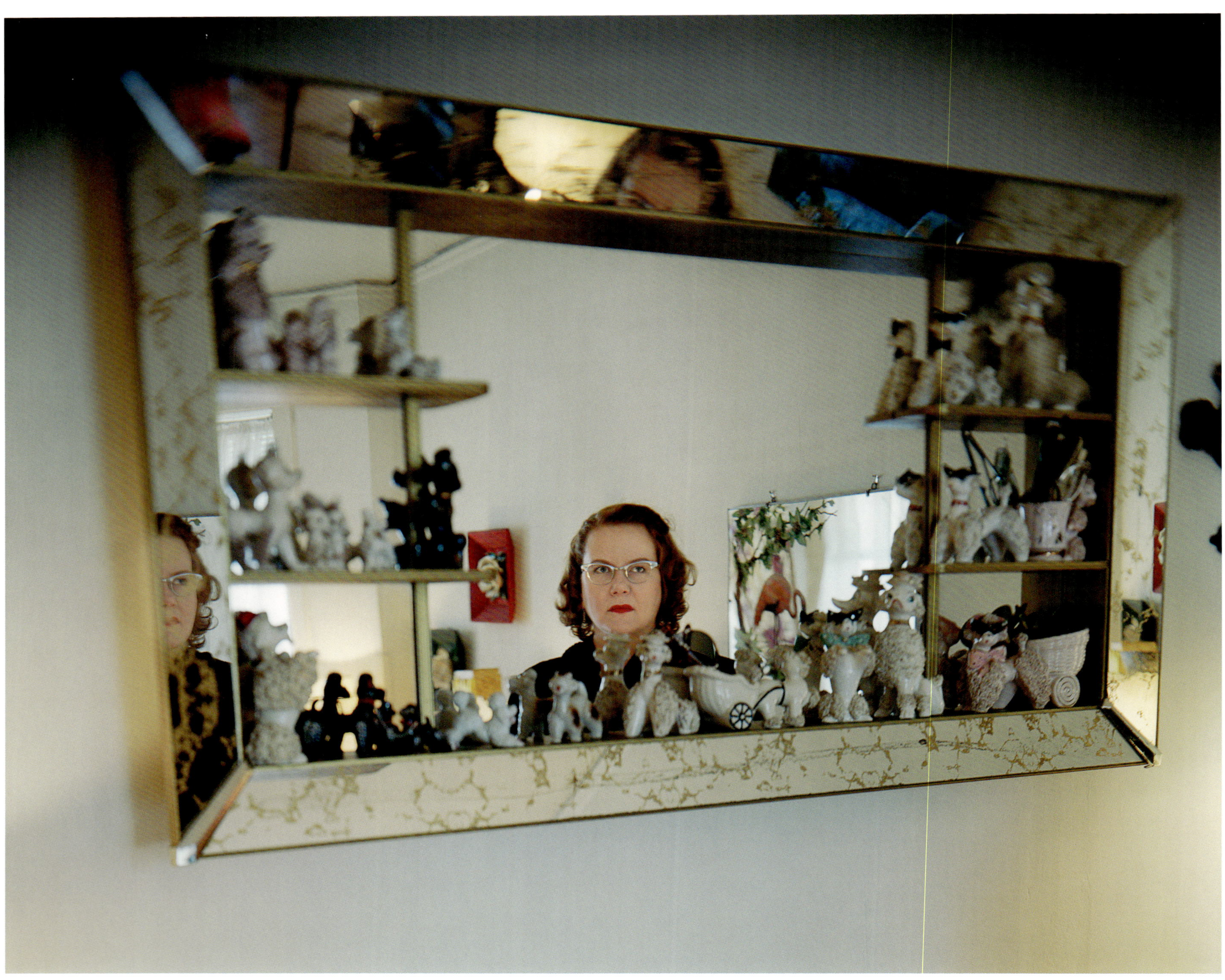

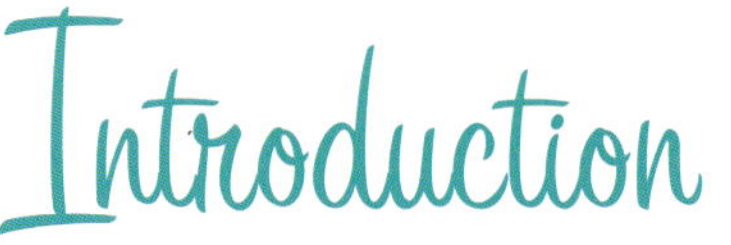

Introduction

by Jennifer Greenburg

MY GRANDPARENTS LIVED IN CHICAGO'S HYDE PARK in a glamorous building called Jackson Towers at the time I was born. It was a building that had two-story apartments, with an Art Deco lobby befitting Joan Crawford, and it overlooked the Museum of Science and Industry, which was originally the Palace of Fine Arts in the 1893 World's Columbian Exposition. It was in my grandparents's classic pre-war apartment that I fell in love with the look of the 1940s and 1950s. My grandmother would hand me a train case filled with Bakelite bangles and costume jewelry—which I much preferred to traditional toys—to play with while I was visiting. I would try on each piece and then wander over to the credenza to look at one of the many black-and-white photographs, which depicted different moments in my grandparents' lives. The photographs of my grandmother as a flapper, of their trip to Cuba in the 1950s, of their meeting place on Douglas Boulevard, and, most significantly, of them dancing at my father's bar mitzvah all transported me to a time period—to a life—I dreamed of living. The images were awash with happiness. I hated to give back the train case when it was time to go home, so I began, at age four, collecting vintage jewelry and clothing. My first purchase was made at a yard sale at the Wrigley Mansion on Chicago's exclusive Astor Street. I bought a pair of 1940s magenta and violet rhinestone chandelier earrings and a faux diamond ring the size of the one Richard Burton gave to Elizabeth Taylor. It came in a celluloid box lined with red velvet.

My interest in the old photographs of my family and the designs of the past allowed me to be the architect of a dream world constructed entirely in my imagination. I would hear the music I thought might accompany the scenes in the vintage photographs. I could imagine the wild music that lead up to the birth of rock and roll. I could see the smoky clubs and imagine the dance floor. As a young girl, I heard songs on the

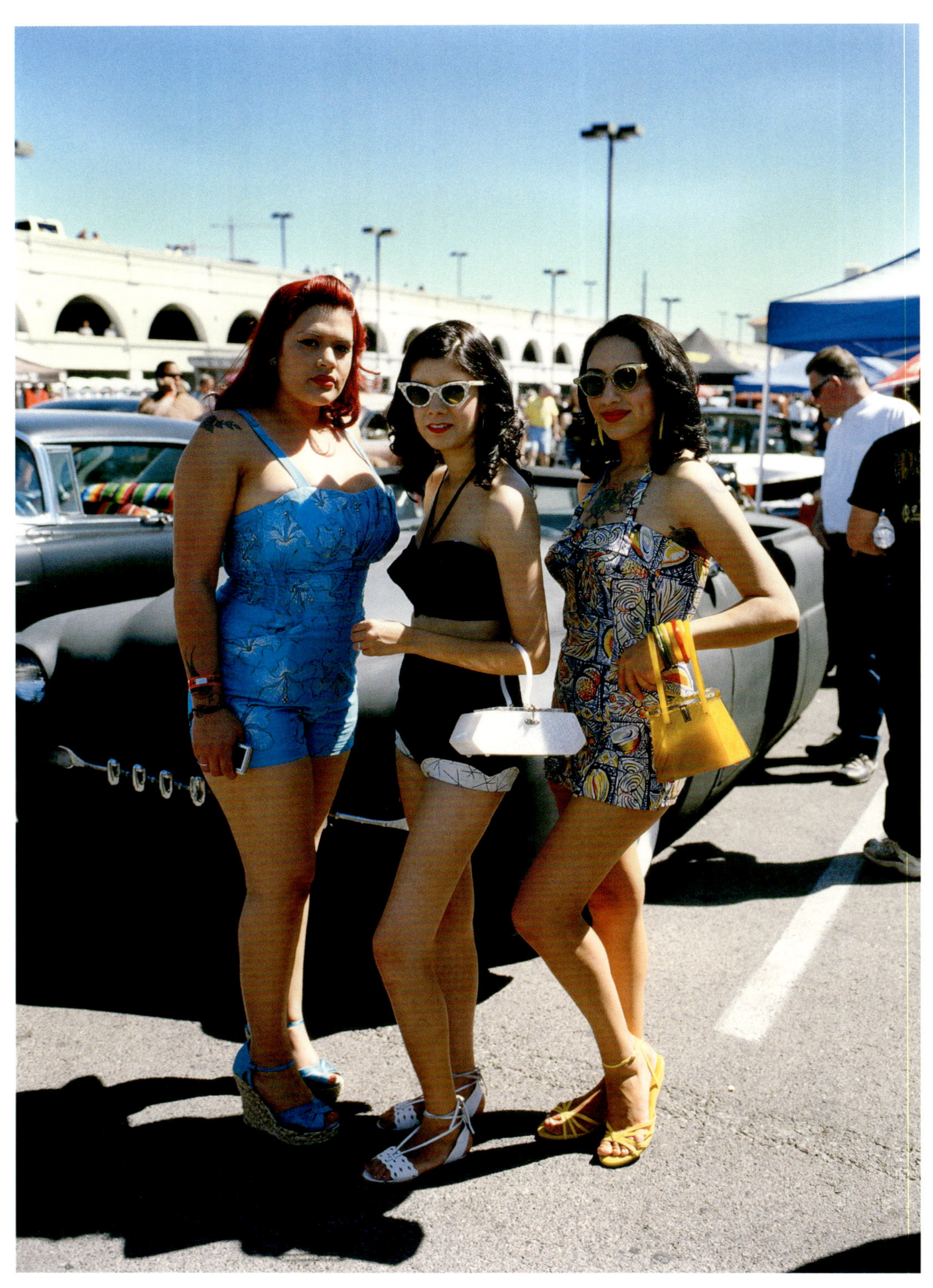

radio by acts like The Stray Cats, but I had no idea how to categorize their music or that there was a rockabilly revival going on in the early 1980s. At age fourteen, I went to a concert at Chicago's Aragon Ballroom. The Aragon claims that more than fifty million people danced in its ballroom to the best orchestras between 1926 and 1955, and you can indeed feel the history inside the building. The ceiling replicates a starry sky, and ornate balconies provide vistas around the marble column covered room. Ironically, beginning in the 1970s, the Aragon became the home of punk rock and rock and roll concerts, which is how I ended up there to see Morrissey on a night when the opening act was quickly replaced by a band called The Planet Rockers. When The Planet Rockers took the stage in metallic sharkskin jackets with animal print lapels, crepe-soled brothel creepers, and an upright bass player, I was awestruck and overcome with delightful glee. The music sounded like the old-time, wild rock and roll I was so desperately seeking, but the players (Eddie Angel, Sonny George, and Mike Winchester) were standing on stage, in front of me, playing live. I had finally found what I was looking for! When I looked around at the crowd, I noticed hundreds of men with pompadours and women in horn-rimmed glasses and vintage dresses. Where did all these people come from, I wondered. It took me nearly eight years to find them again and to join their ranks.

In the summer of 2001, I had just completed a M.F.A at the University of Chicago. My thesis (in the form of images, text, and video) had been about my single girlfriends who were transitioning, kicking and screaming, into adulthood. There was a freedom and whimsy about the post-college/grad life that interested me. Everyone was savoring his or her last irresponsible moments. And something was changing rapidly in the country. A president, who had not been elected to office by the public vote, was appointed by the U.S. Supreme Court to govern our nation. Mediocrity and religious fundamentalism began to be celebrated. 9/11 happened and the U.S. waged a xenophobic "war on terror." And the country, in my opinion, entered a new and bleak time period. As an artist and a liberal—in fact, as a human being—I felt defeated and hopeless. All I wanted was to escape into the vivid world depicted in my grandmother's photographs.

I was spending weekends—now that I had time outside of my studies—at farm sales, vintage-inspired music events, and vintage clothing sales. While out, I began to see people my own age dressed as I was, in clothing from the 1940s and 1950s. I had seen some of these people at concerts and remembered the likes of some from the Morrissey concert eight years before, but I had never had the opportunity to speak to any of them. My friends in college and graduate school barely cared about vintage music or fashion and tended to think of my interests as boring or weird. I had a habit of begging everyone I knew to go to a concert or drive with me sixty miles to shop an antique sale. Rarely was anyone willing, so I went to many places by myself. I craved friends who were interested in old rock and roll and vintage clothing, accessories, and furnishings. Eventually, people at the sales began to recognize me as a serious collector and enthusiast, and our conversations and friendships began. I was finally accepted as someone who was more than just a tourist.

My assumption, at that time, was that my new friends were planning to live what I then believed to be a modern lifestyle driven by career aspirations. I also thought that their interest in vintage articles was merely ephemeral. I discovered, however, that, while we shared the same aesthetic, our perspectives on modern life were very different. Many of my new friends were actively pursuing a 1950s lifestyle of marrying young, moving to the suburbs, and having children. They did not care much for the ins and outs of politics (at least at the time), and they weren't losing sleep over the economy, AIDS, or *Roe v. Wade.* I had found a subculture of people who mostly turned away from the horrors of contemporary American culture to focus on family, friends, music, and vintage Americana. I was hooked, jealous, and fascinated all at the same time. It was like this subculture had heard my cries and materialized at the moment I needed a shining light.

The idea of photographing the rockabilly subculture occurred to me when one of my girlfriends, who had initially been part of my thesis series of young women, became pregnant, got married, and moved to the suburbs, all within a short period of time. She had gone from being the girl with a pixie haircut, who rode her bike from bar to bar, to become a 1950s blonde bombshell of a housewife. She began wearing vintage clothing and coiffing herself like someone out of *Life* magazine. She was transformed practically overnight. It is her transformation that I captured in the first image in *The Rockabillies,* "Angie & Kleen with Butch" (opposite), and with that I embarked on an entirely new chapter in my life and career.

My friend's metamorphosis made it clear to me that being part of this subculture was more than just fashion; it is a way of life. To some, this way of life might seem anachronistic, with its carefully codified aesthetic. But, the subcultural community in general, and the rockabilly community, for me personally, have taken the place of religious affiliation in modern life. Rockabillies share a set of visible signifiers in dress and

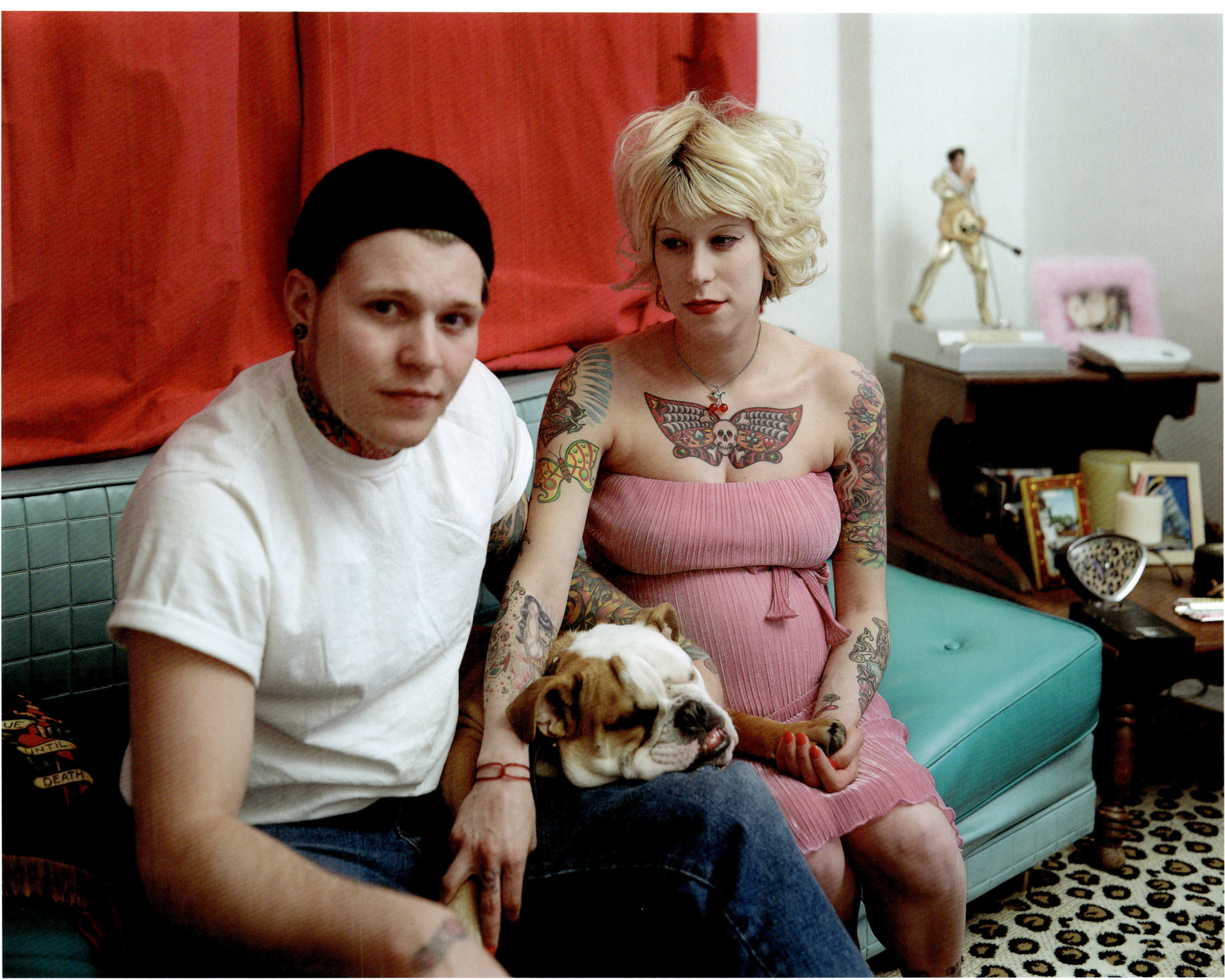

choices of decorative arts, a way of engaging socially, and cultural icons. The ability to easily identify one another in social settings results in a trust that comes from a common belief and value system.

I wondered, at the outset of my work on the series, what was the genesis of the rockabilly subculture? During a lecture I was giving on Edward Steichen's early advertisements for Eastman-Kodak, it became clear to me: the rockabillies have idealized the lifestyle presented in the idealized advertisements and Hollywood films of the 1950s. *Life* and *Look* magazines serve, to most rockabillies, as a record of the way the perfect life must have looked in the 1950s and, more importantly, as a blueprint of the way they want their lives to be now. These sources are, of course, no more real than *Martha Stewart Living* is to today's culture, however; the fantasy is what the rockabillies want, and they are completely aware of it. I caught on to this immediately because I, too, wanted to live that same fantasy.

I began going to every rockabilly weekender (music/clothing/car festivals held across the nation) to hear both new and vintage musical acts such as Ronnie Dawson, Janis Martin, Wanda Jackson, Big Sandy & His Fly-Rite Boys, The Extraordinaires, and The Paladins. As I met more people, I was able to make more photographs. I would get to know a person or couple and then travel to their hometown to photograph them. I rarely photographed someone I did not know well. That, much like a kiss on a first date, would have rushed our relationship. Photographing someone, to me, is very intimate. The 4 x 5 view camera that I use forces me to stand face-to-face with my subjects while the exposure is being made. There is no lens to hide behind. I get shy, nervous, and, oddly, quiet. I feel as vulnerable as the person in front of the camera.

The time it took for me to be accepted as a non-tourist in the rockabilly scene taught me something very important about the type of photographs I make. I have always been infuriated by images taken by people who try to uncover a freakish or "other" culture. To me, those photographers are imprinting their judgment all over the film. I do not want to be associated with what I judge to be an exploitative tradition. I want to be fair; I want collaboration between my subjects and myself. I want to make each person into the icon that they truly deserve to be. The time and effort put into cultivating such a lifestyle deserves much more than a passing snapshot. This conviction earned me the full support and participation from the people in the images. I found a community of people who have successfully created their own happiness and community, and it is my pleasure to allow viewers a glimpse of that happiness.

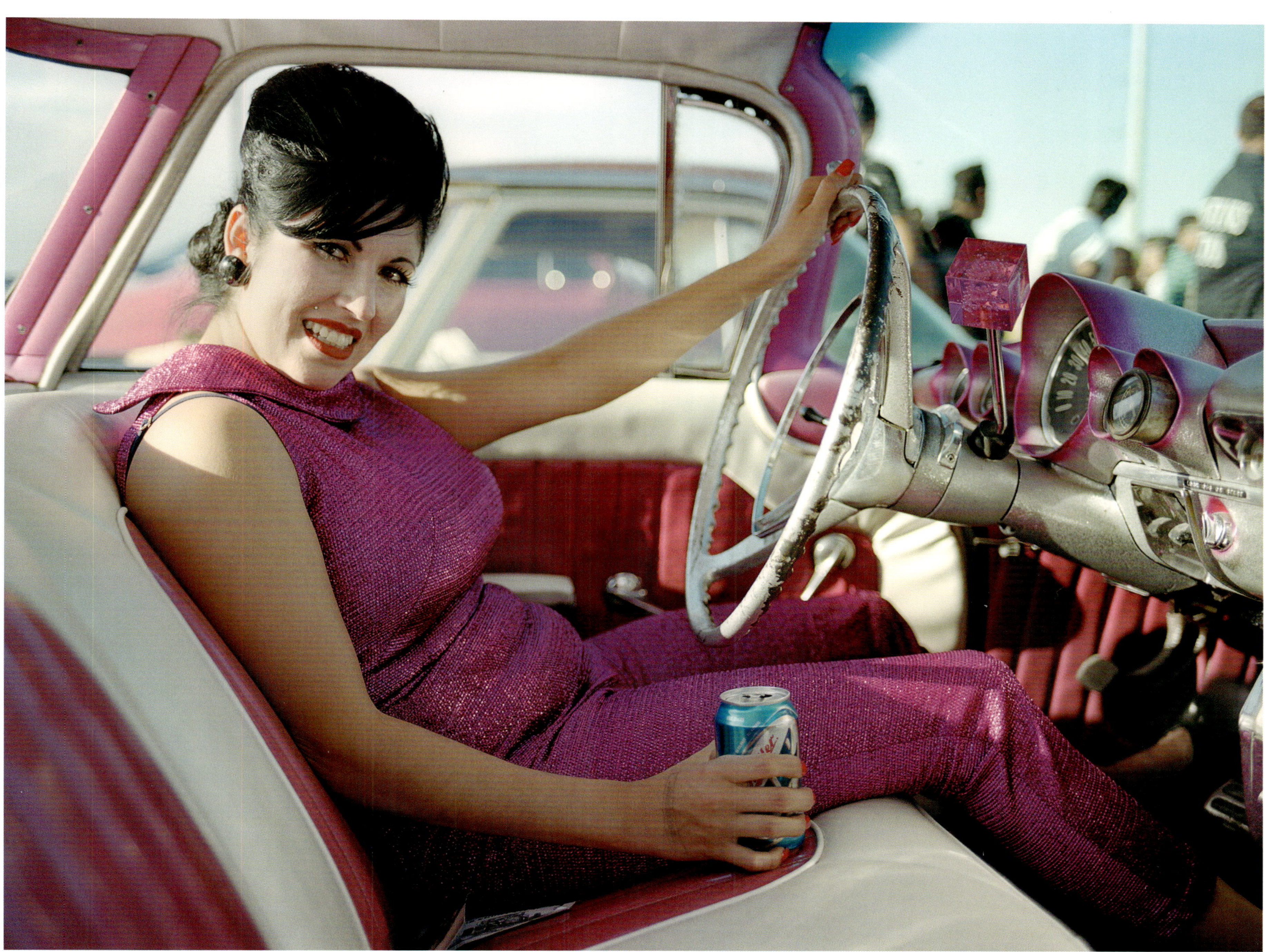

The Rockabillies

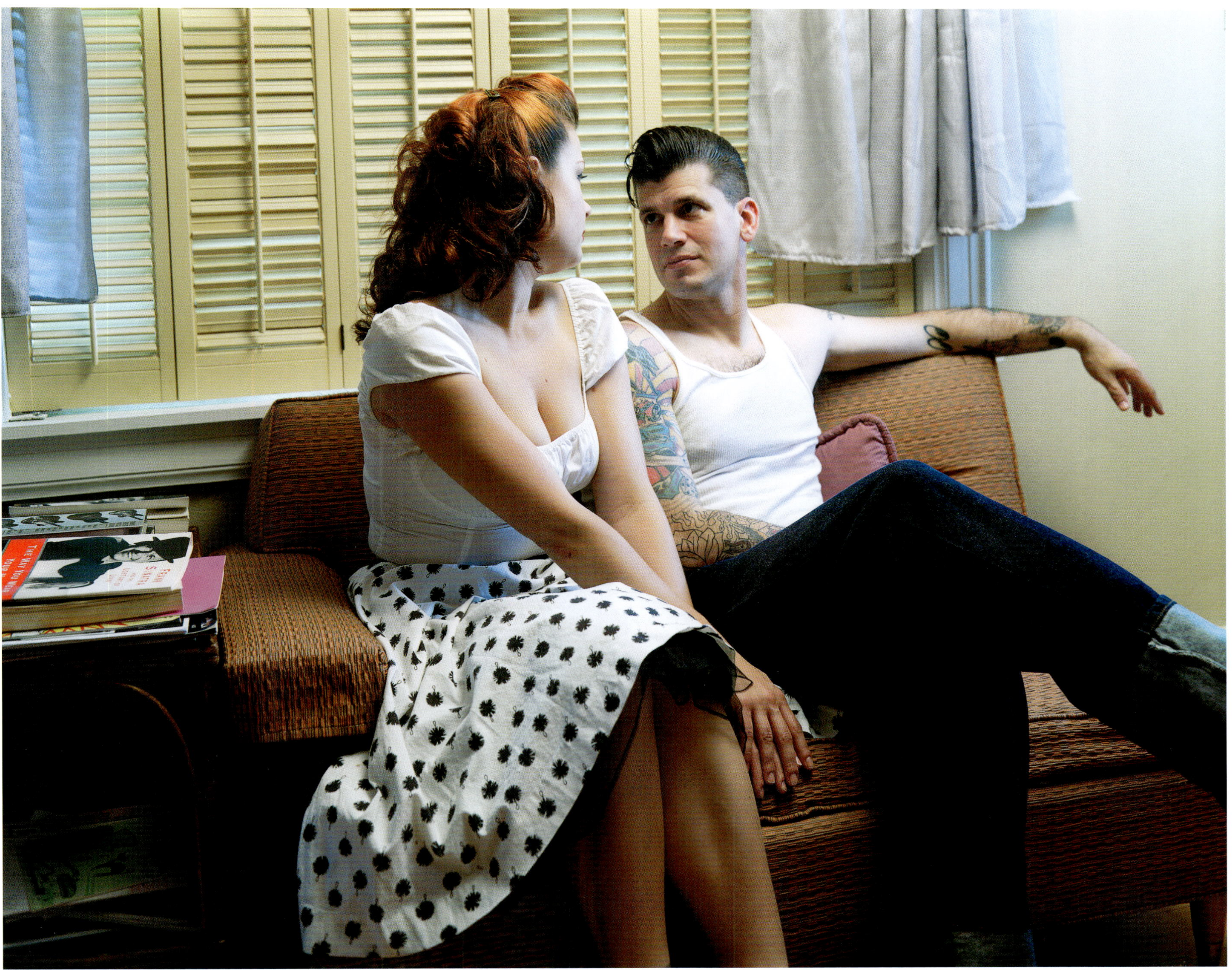

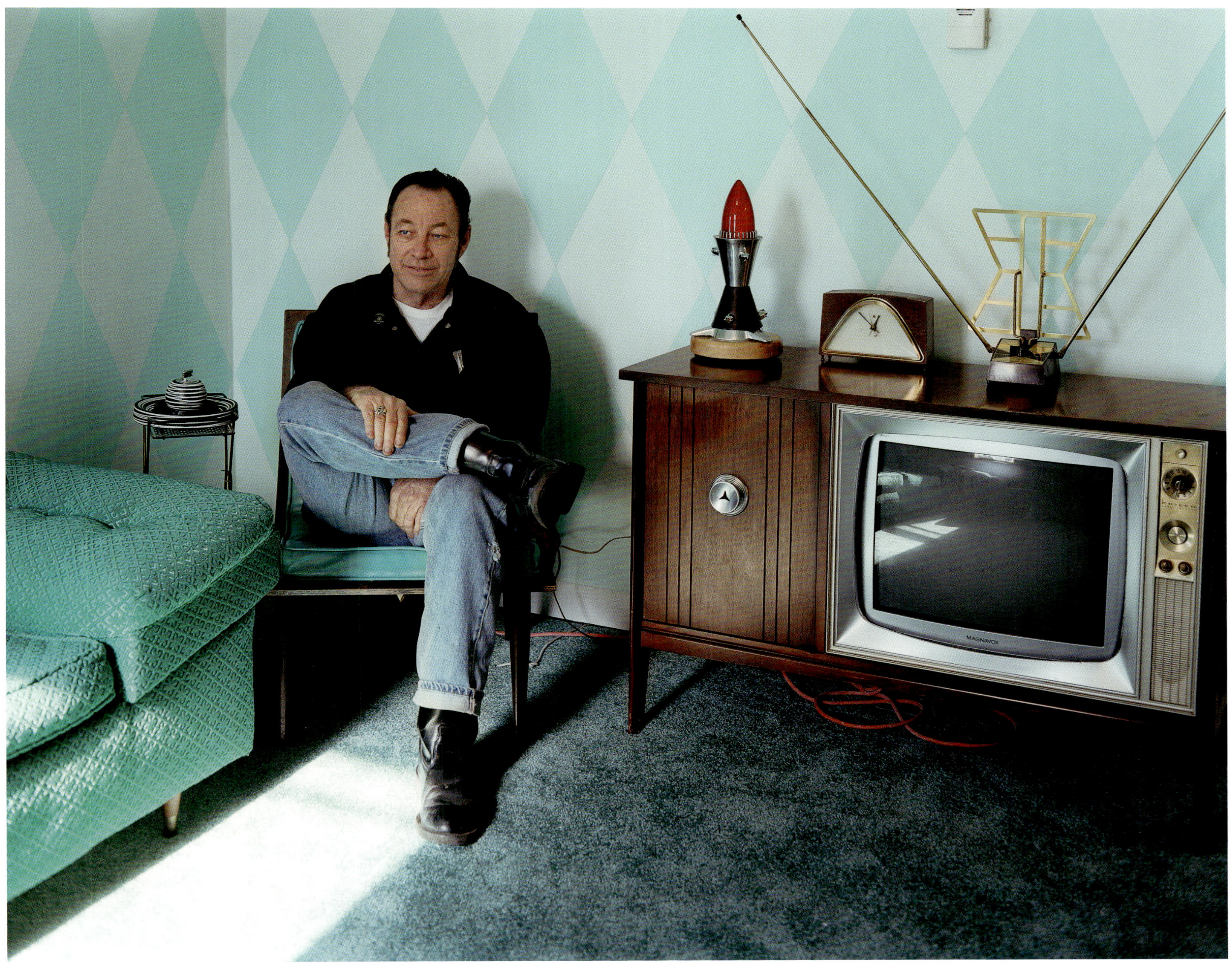

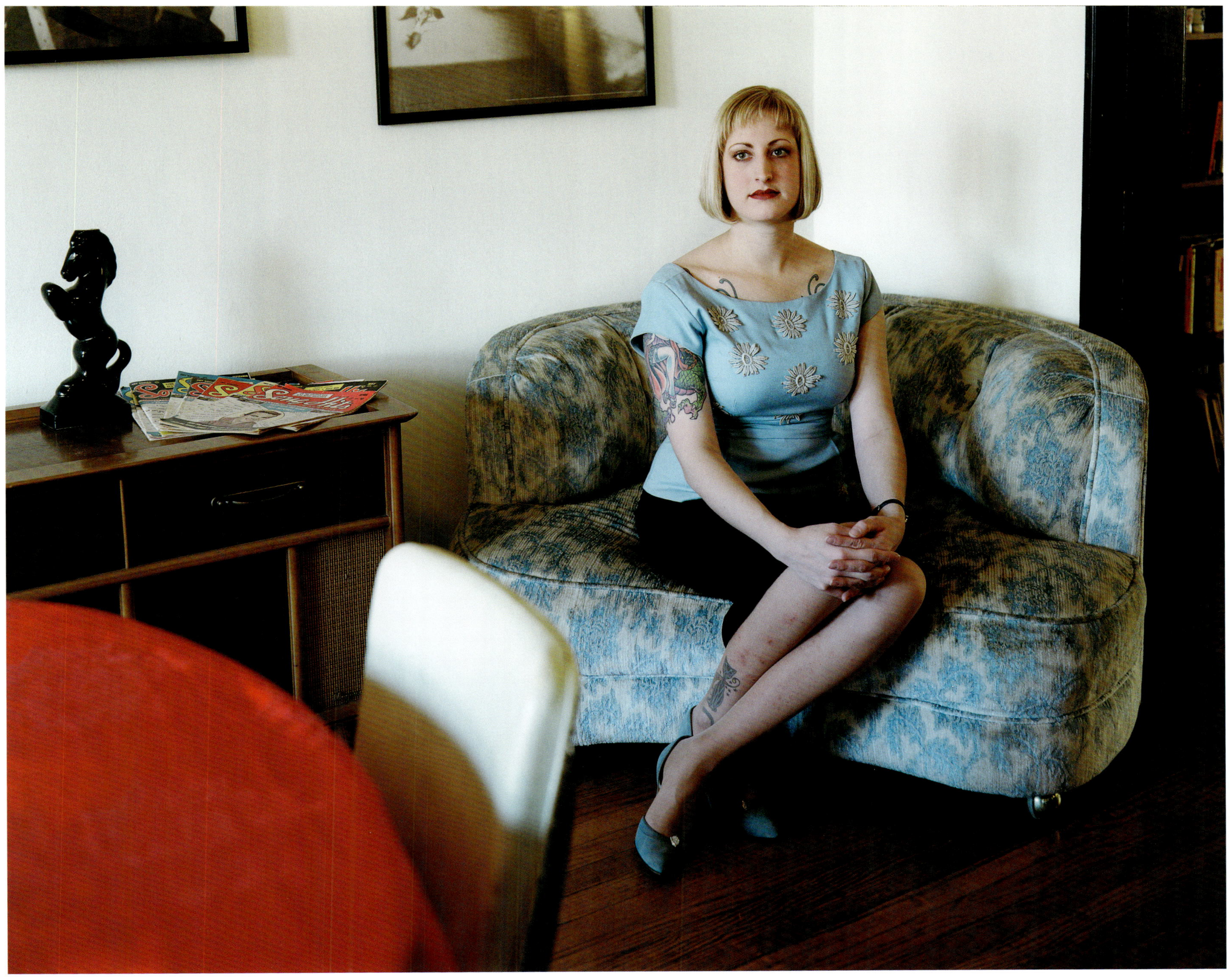

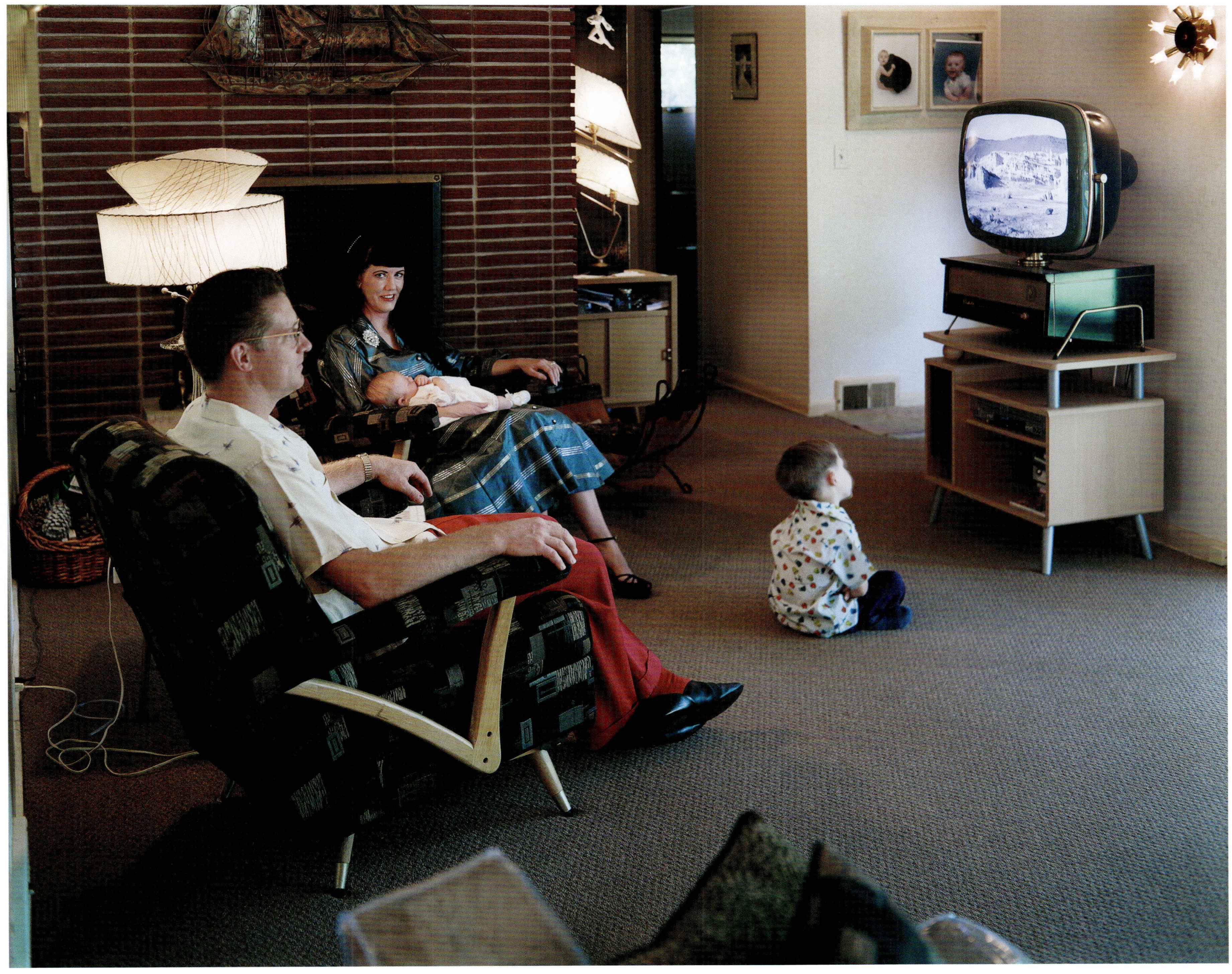

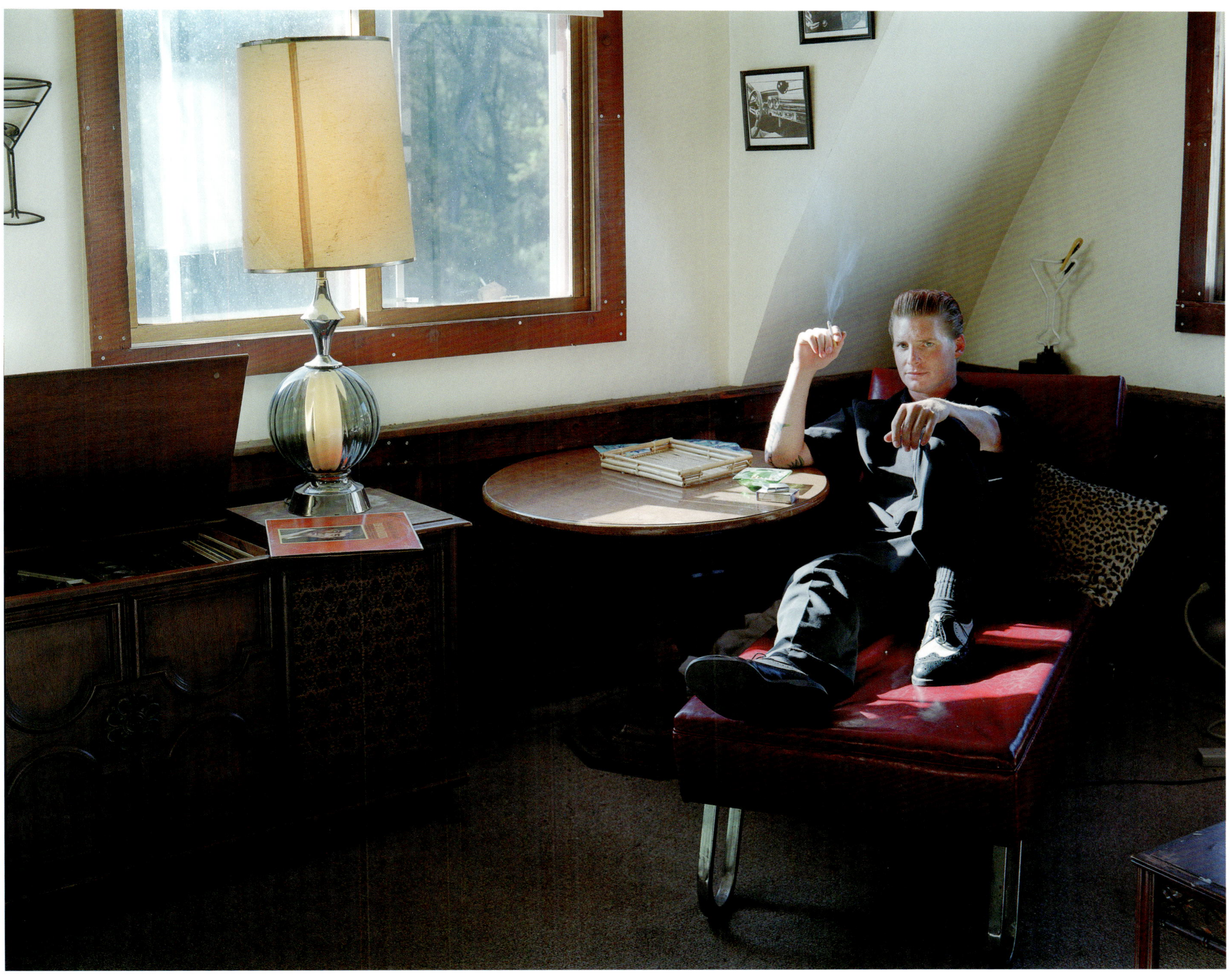

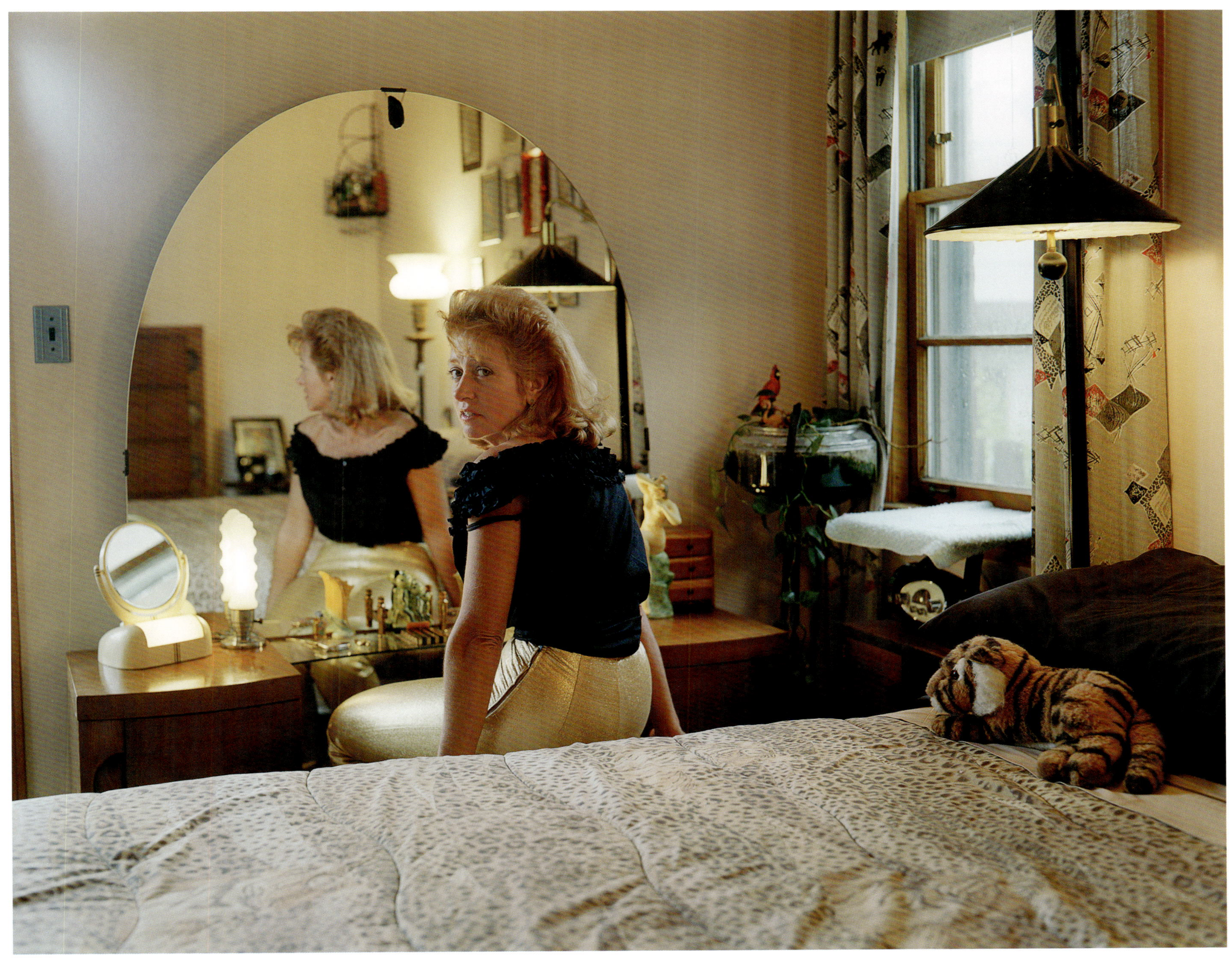

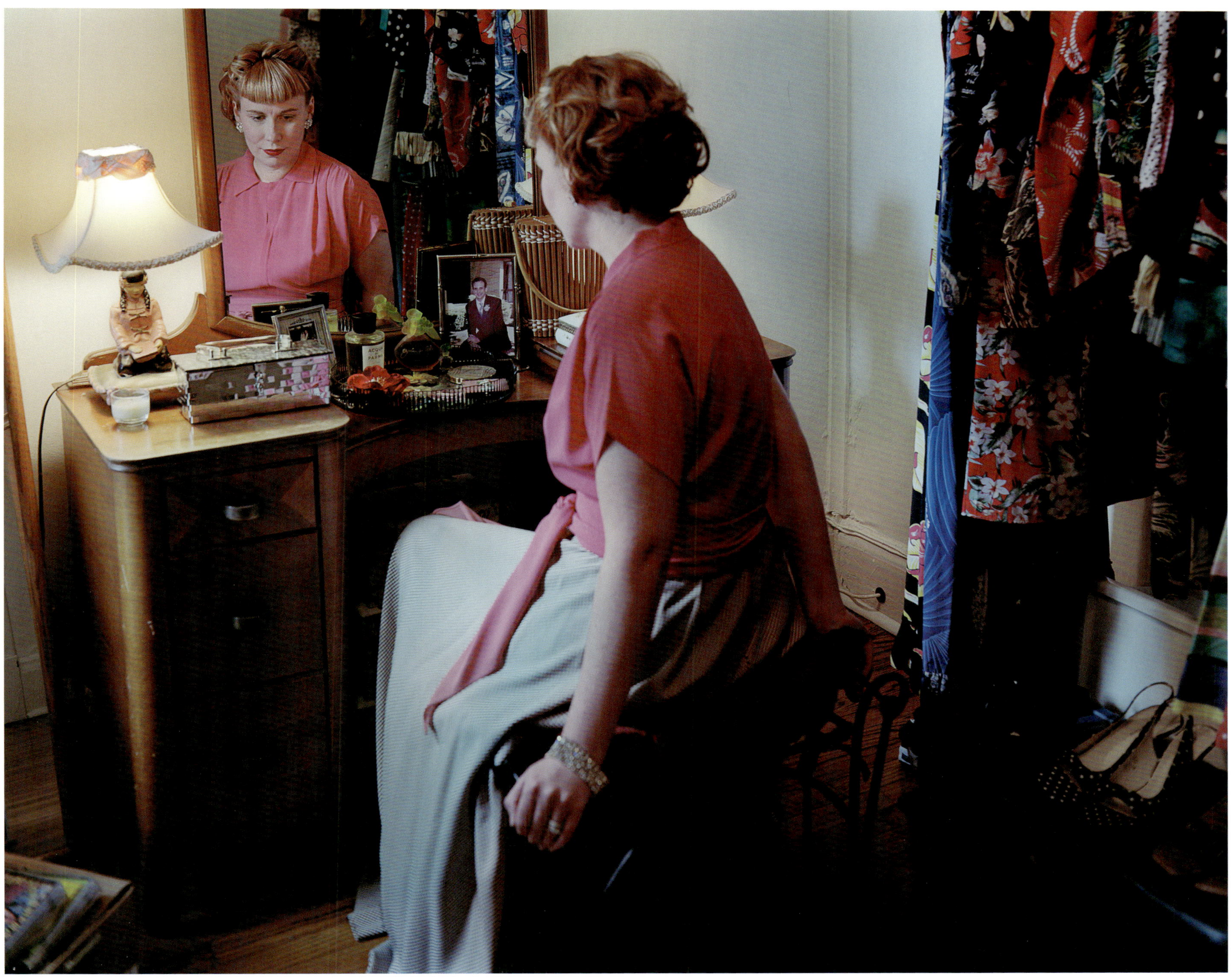

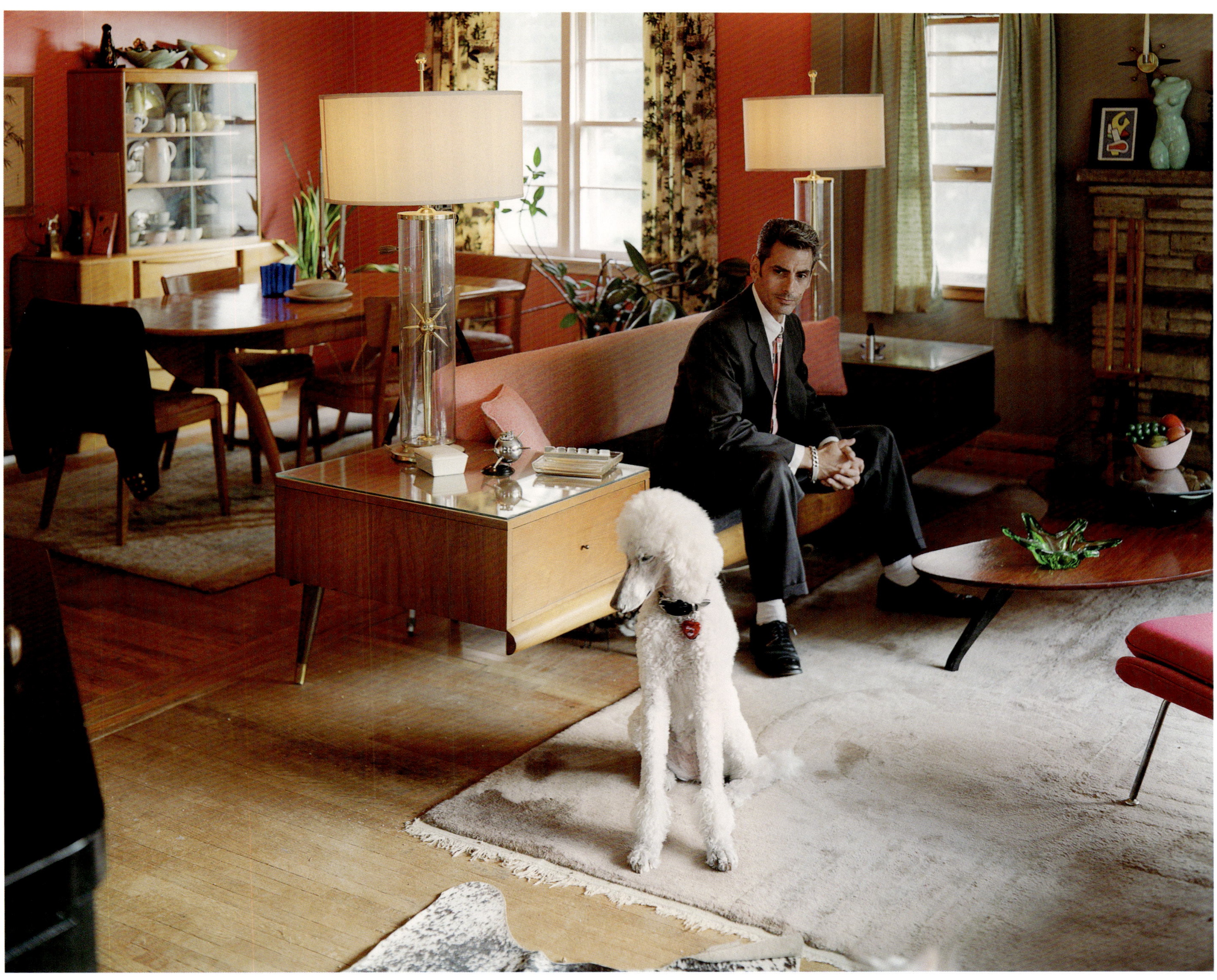

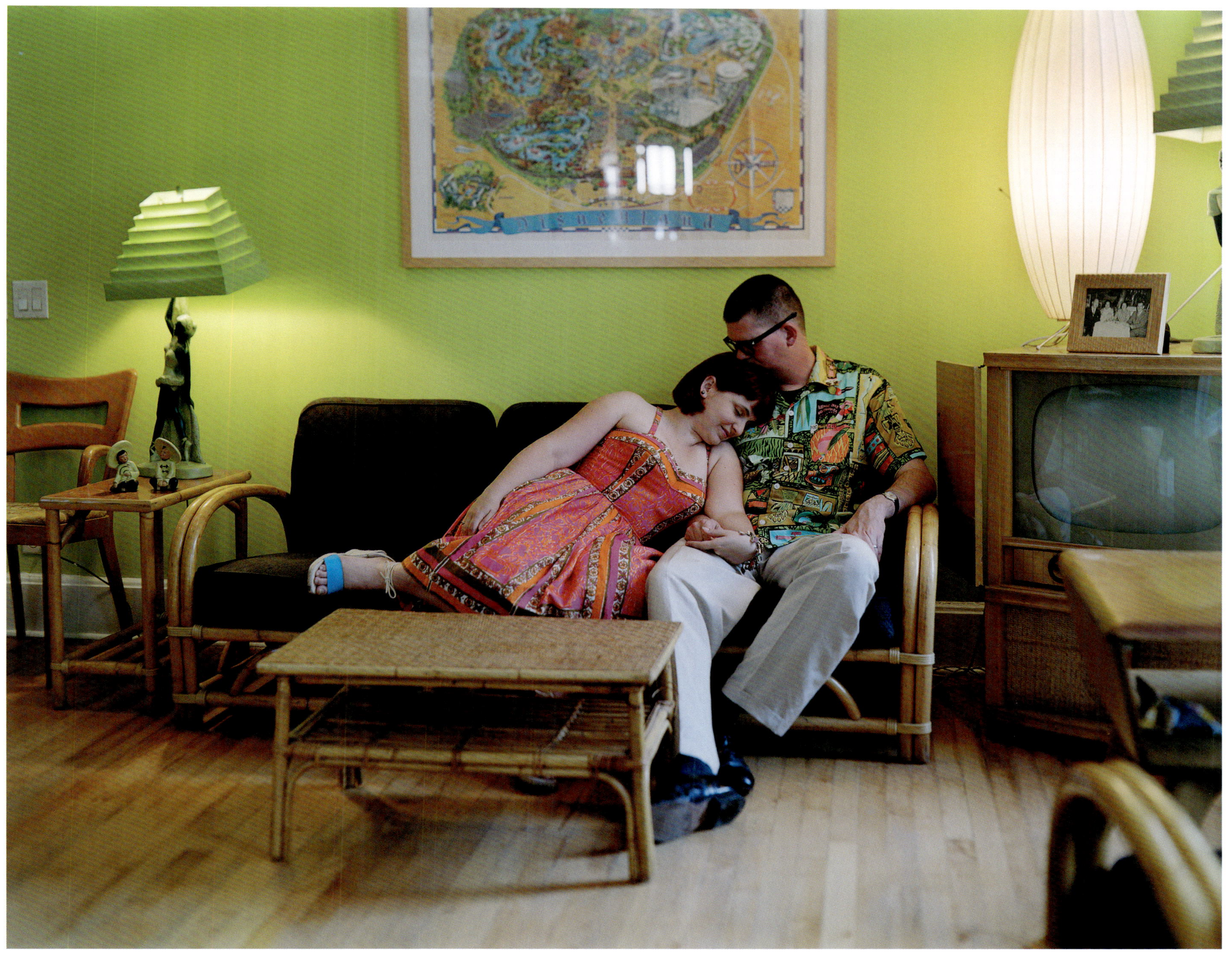

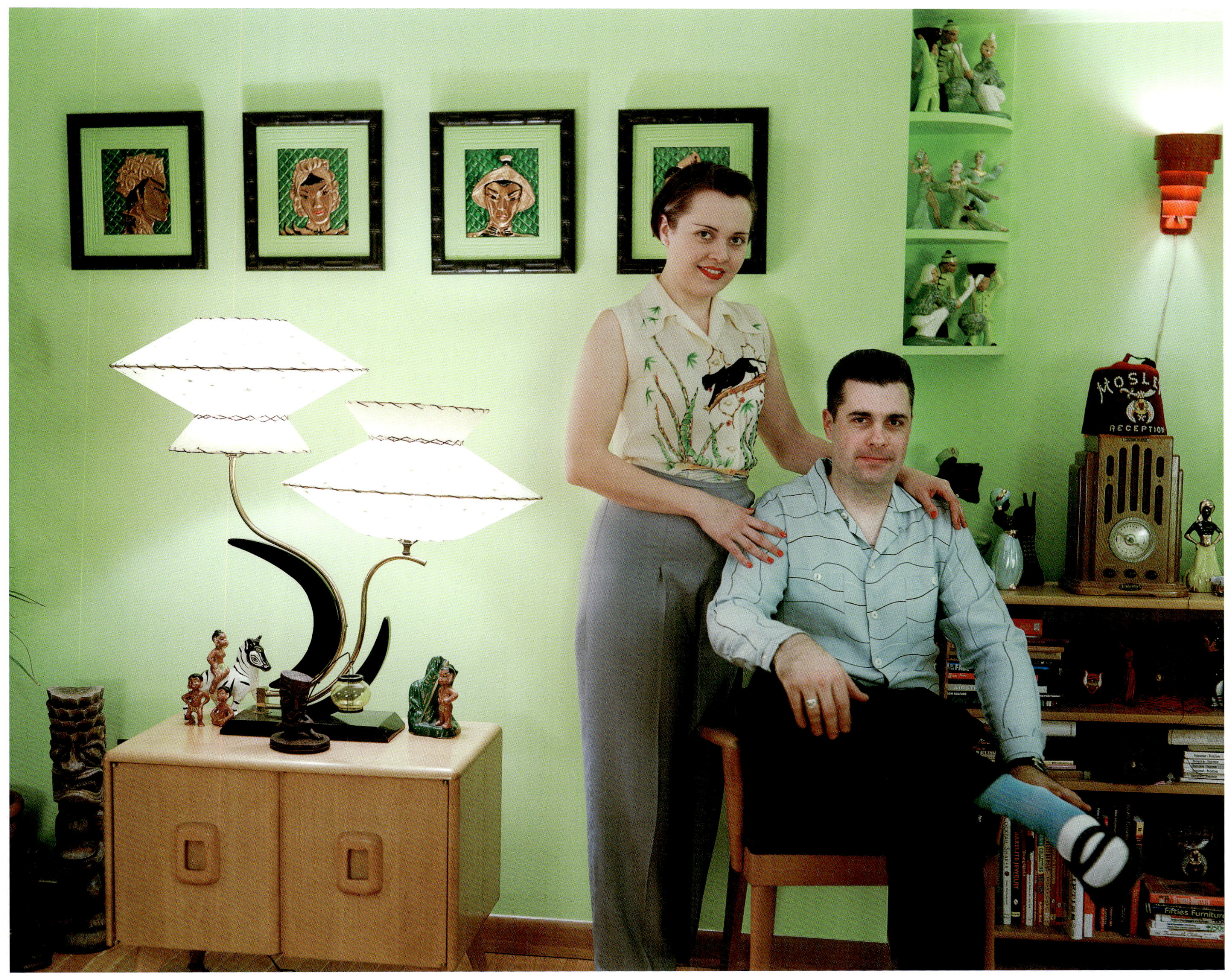

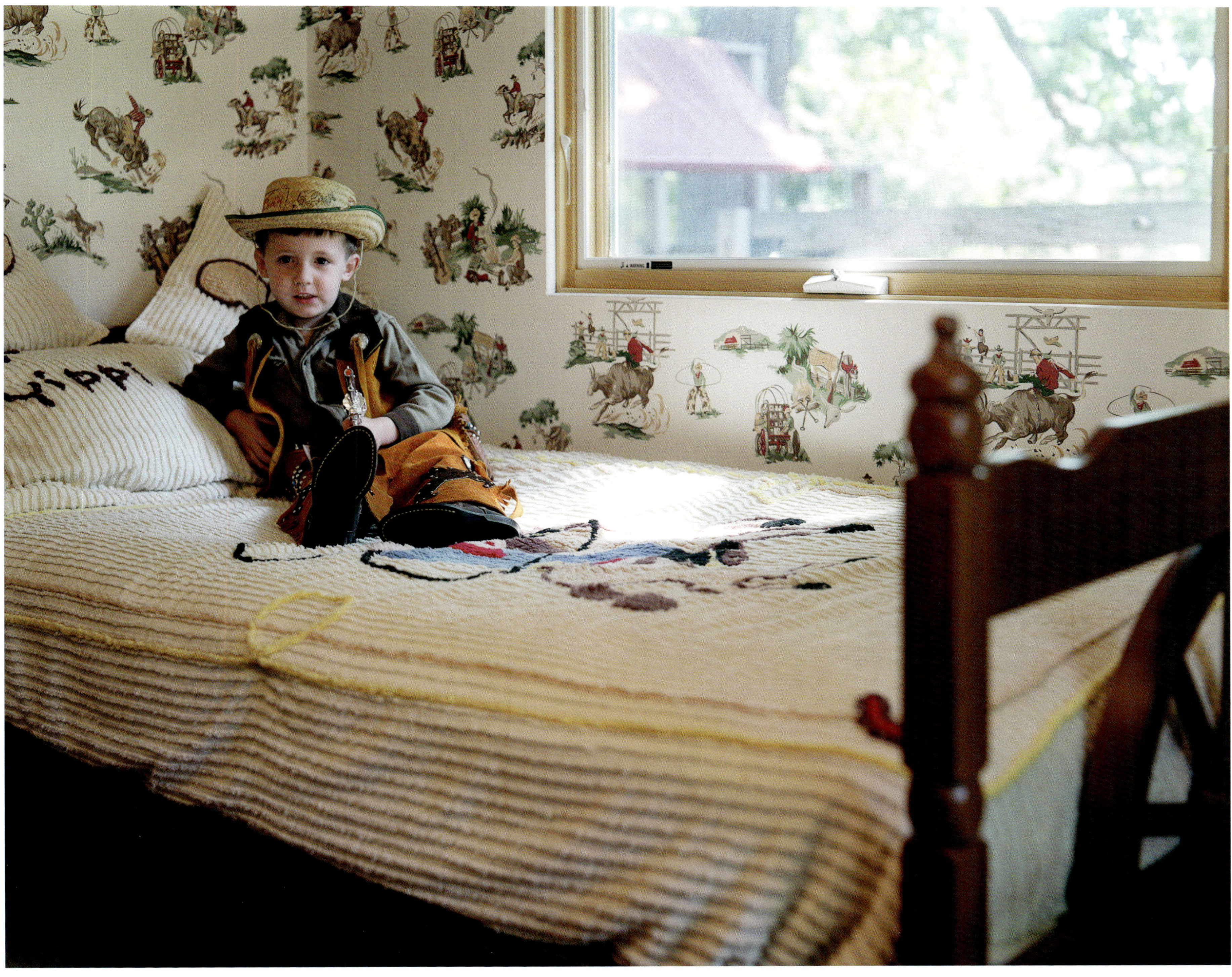

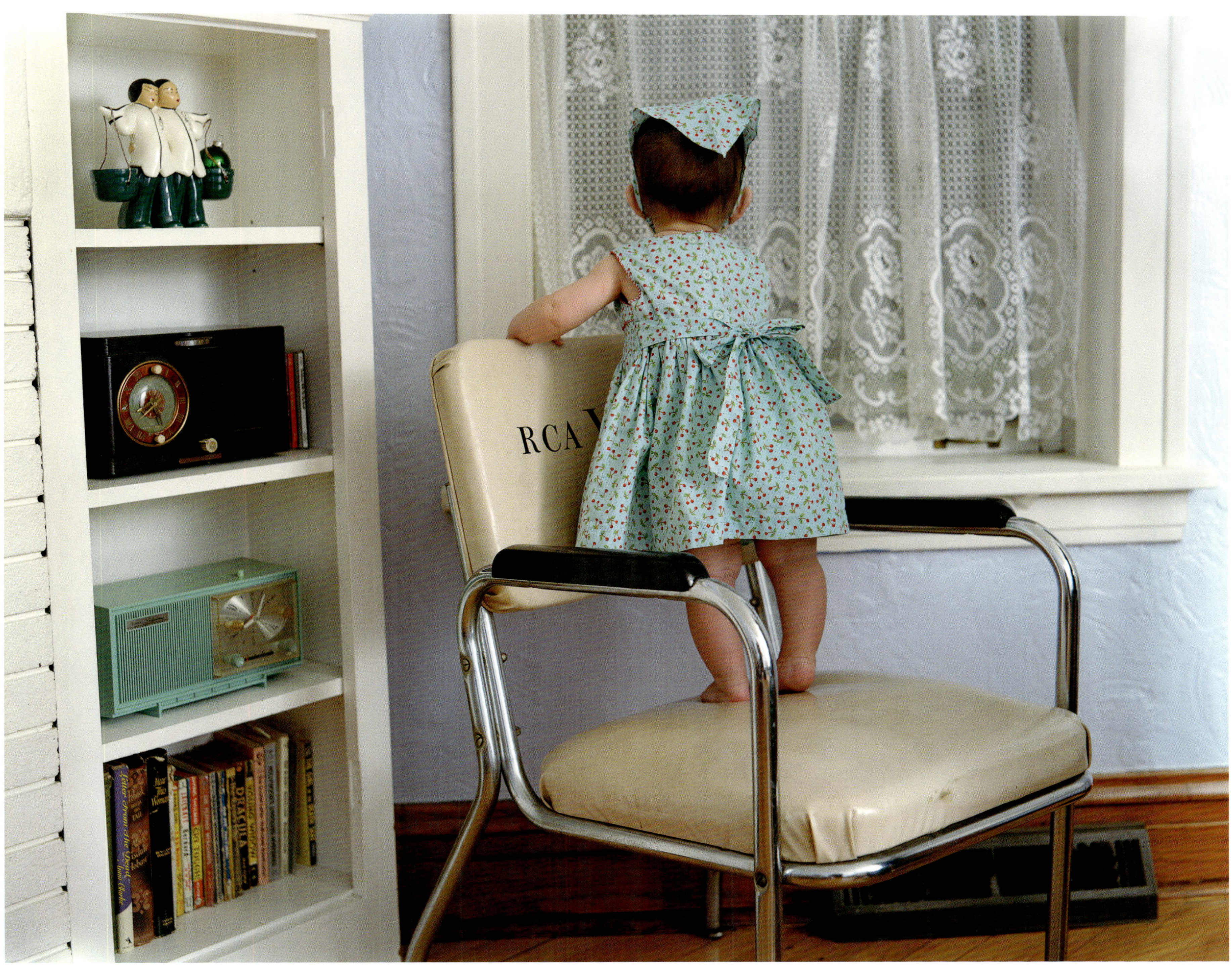

RCA V

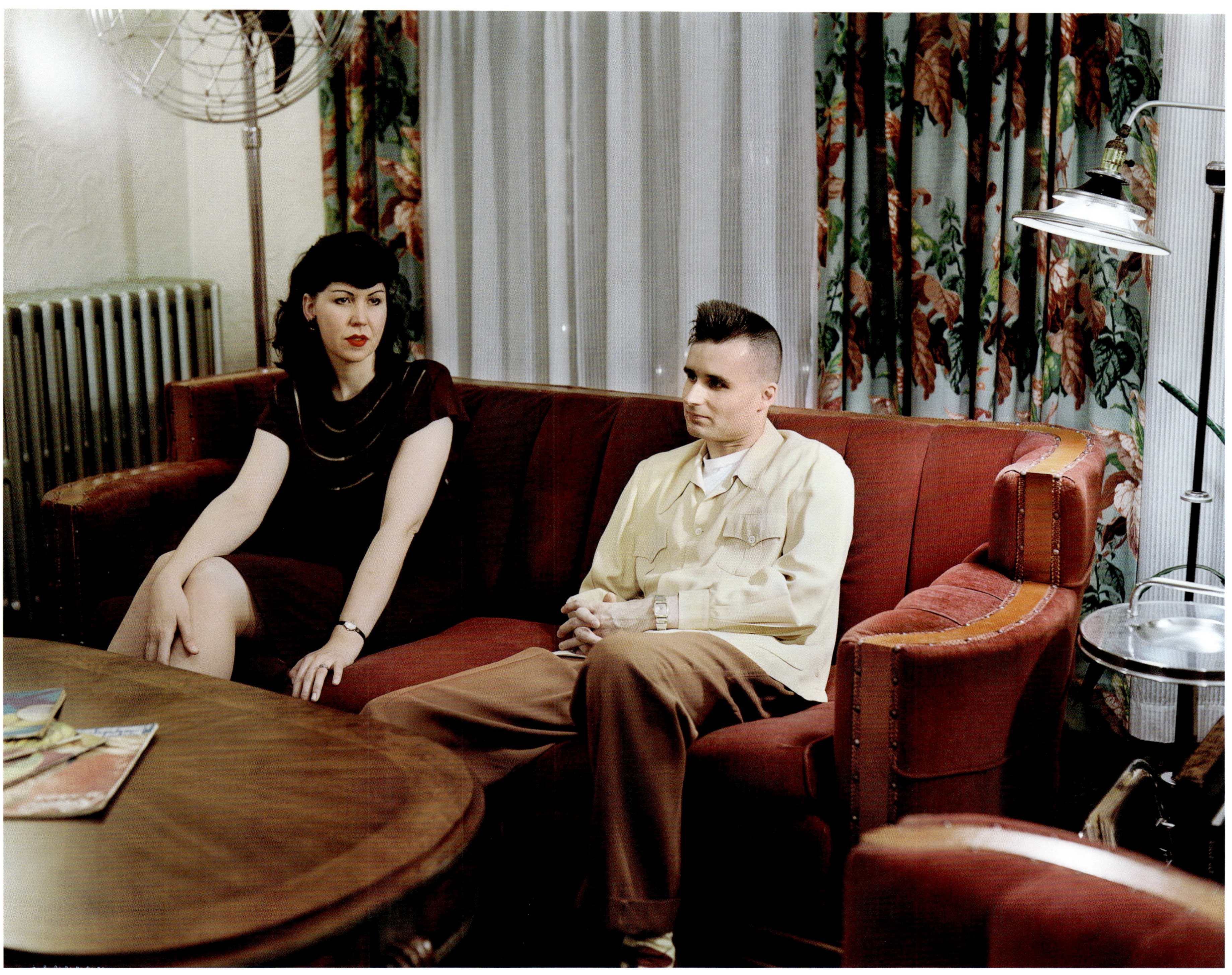

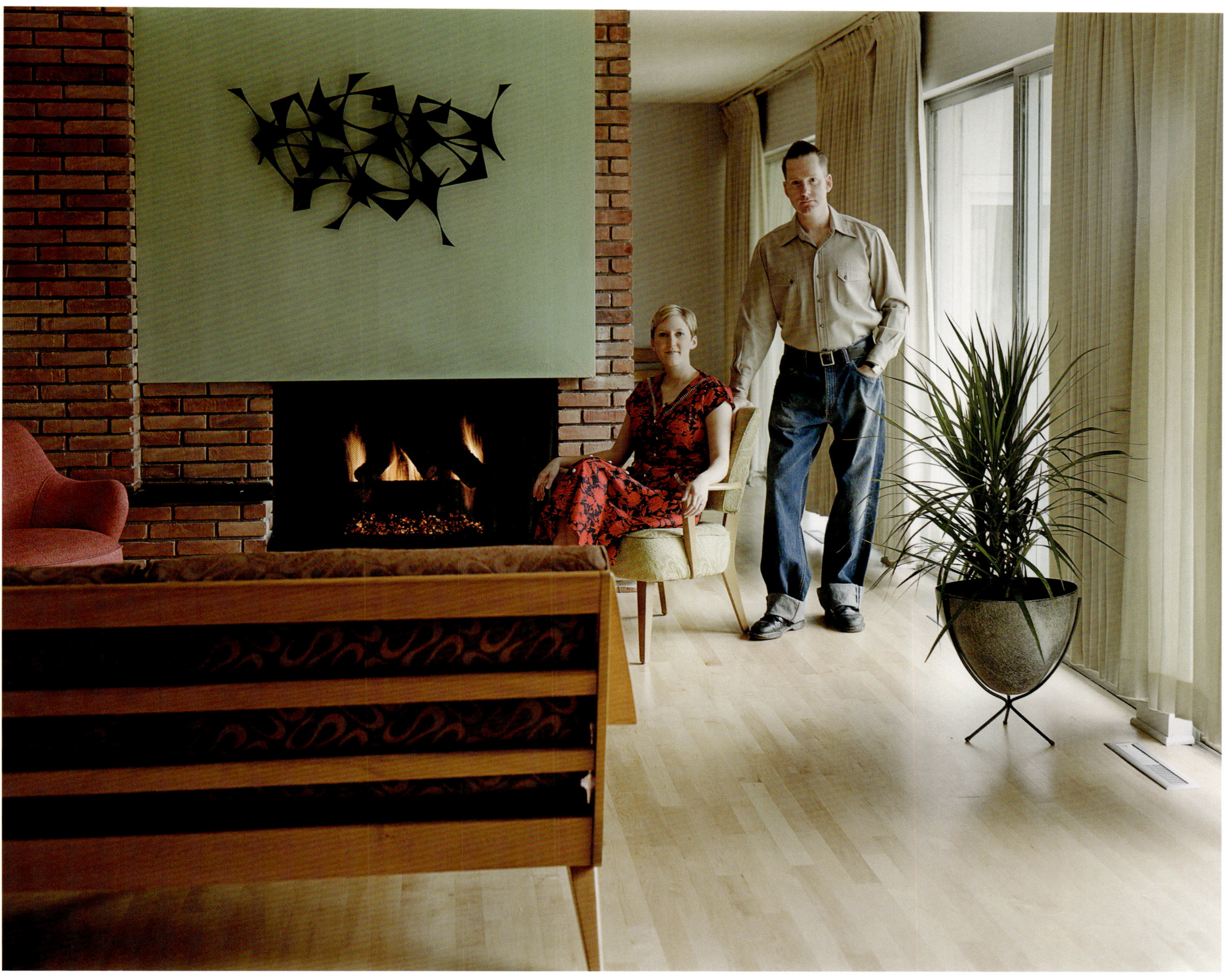

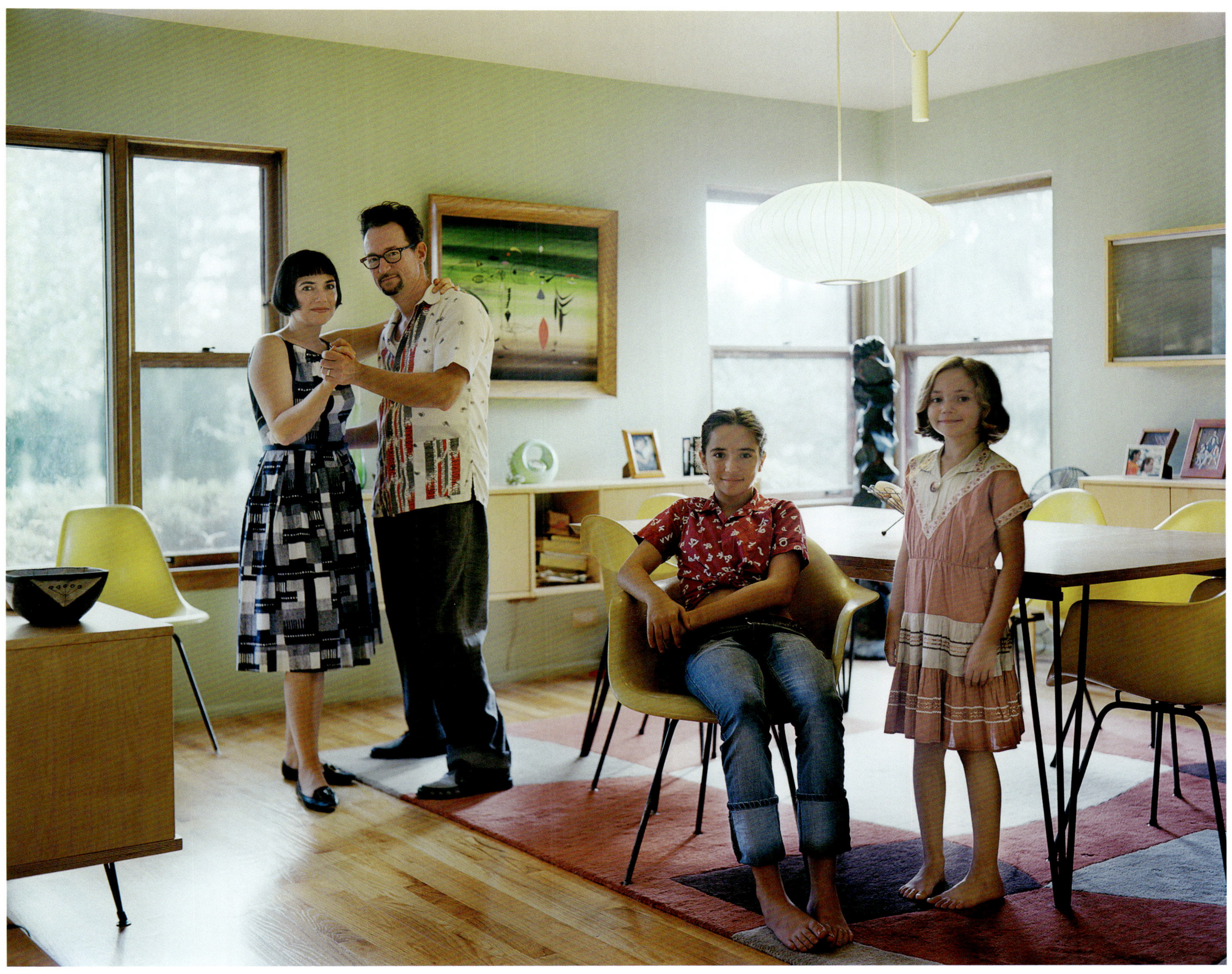

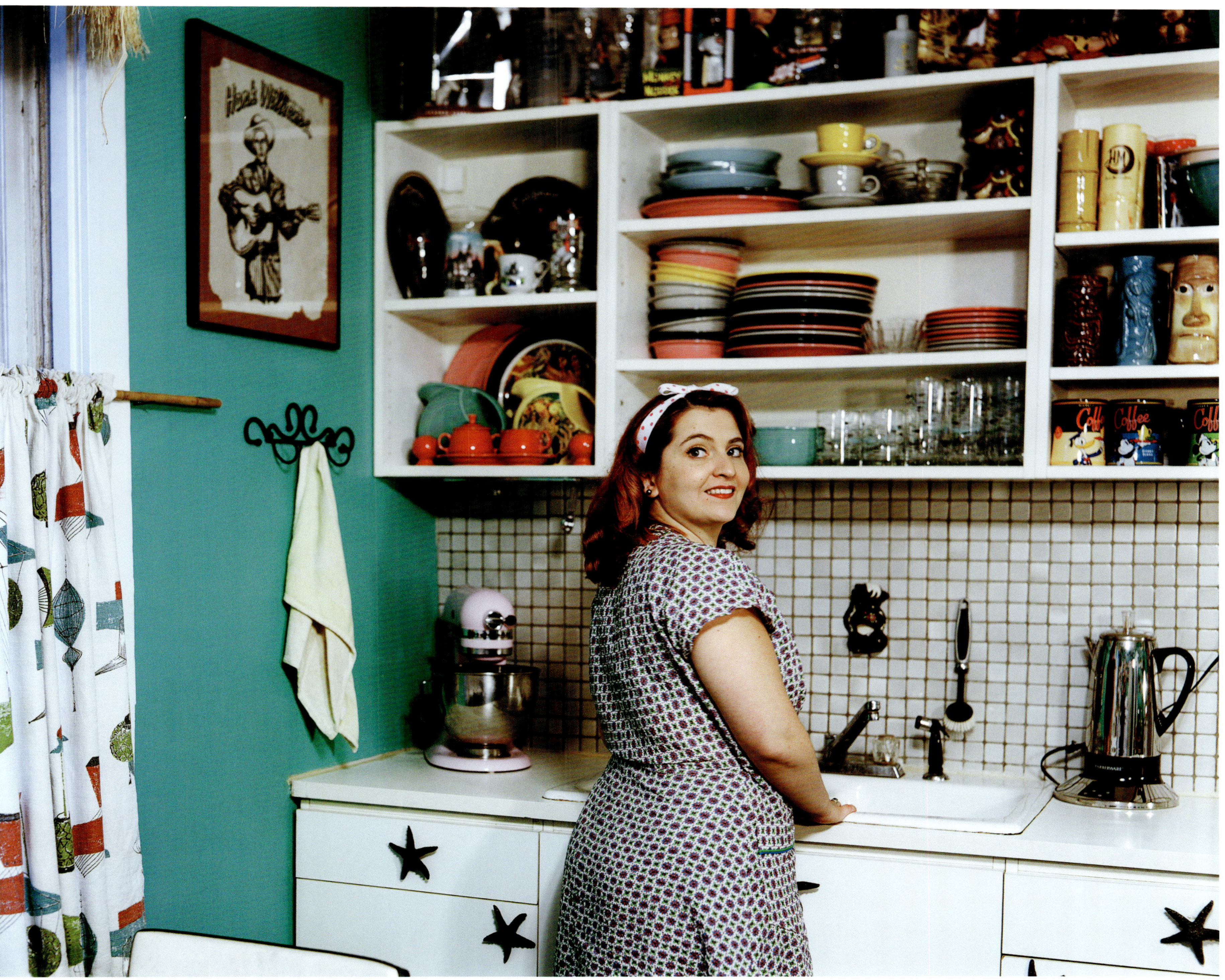

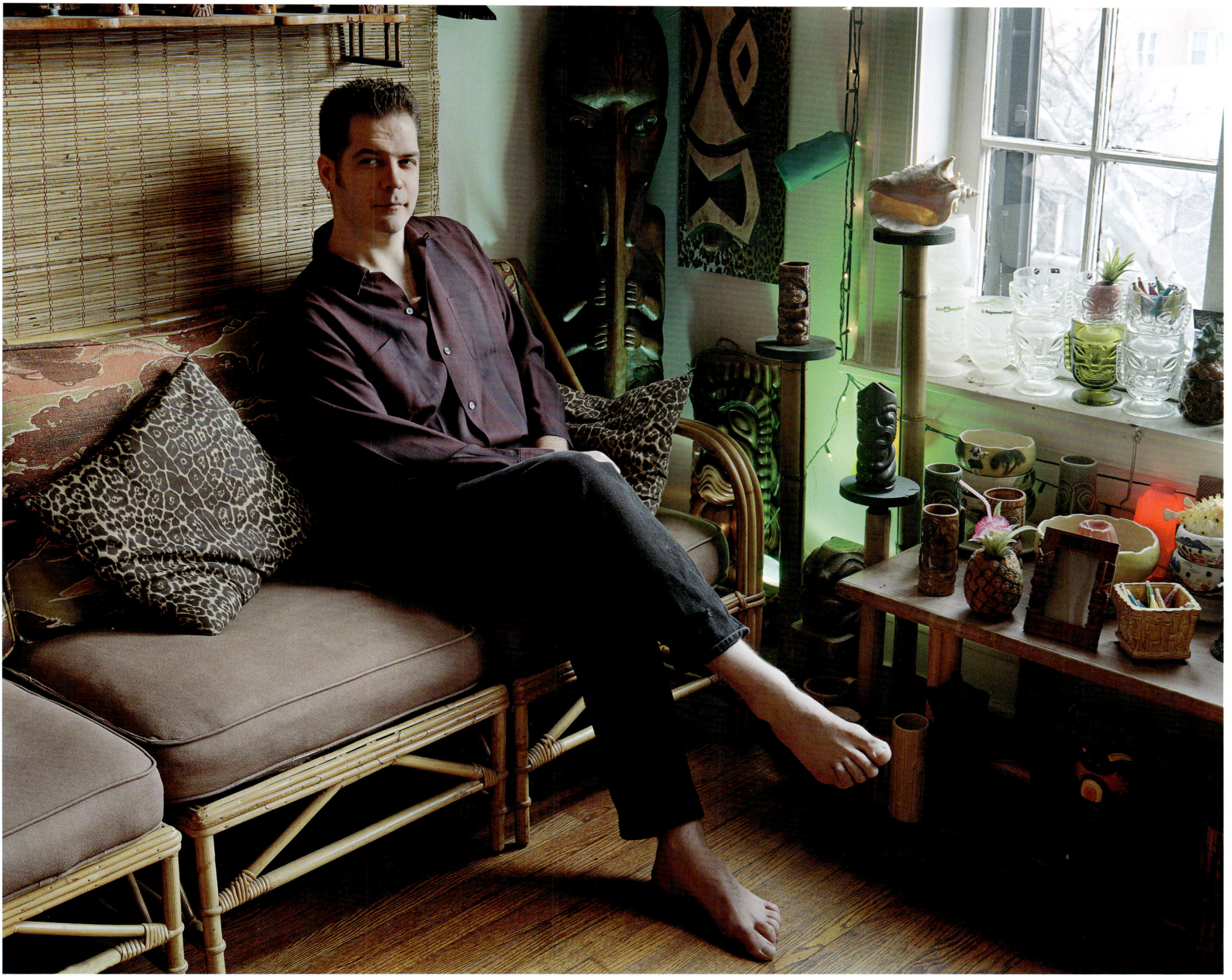

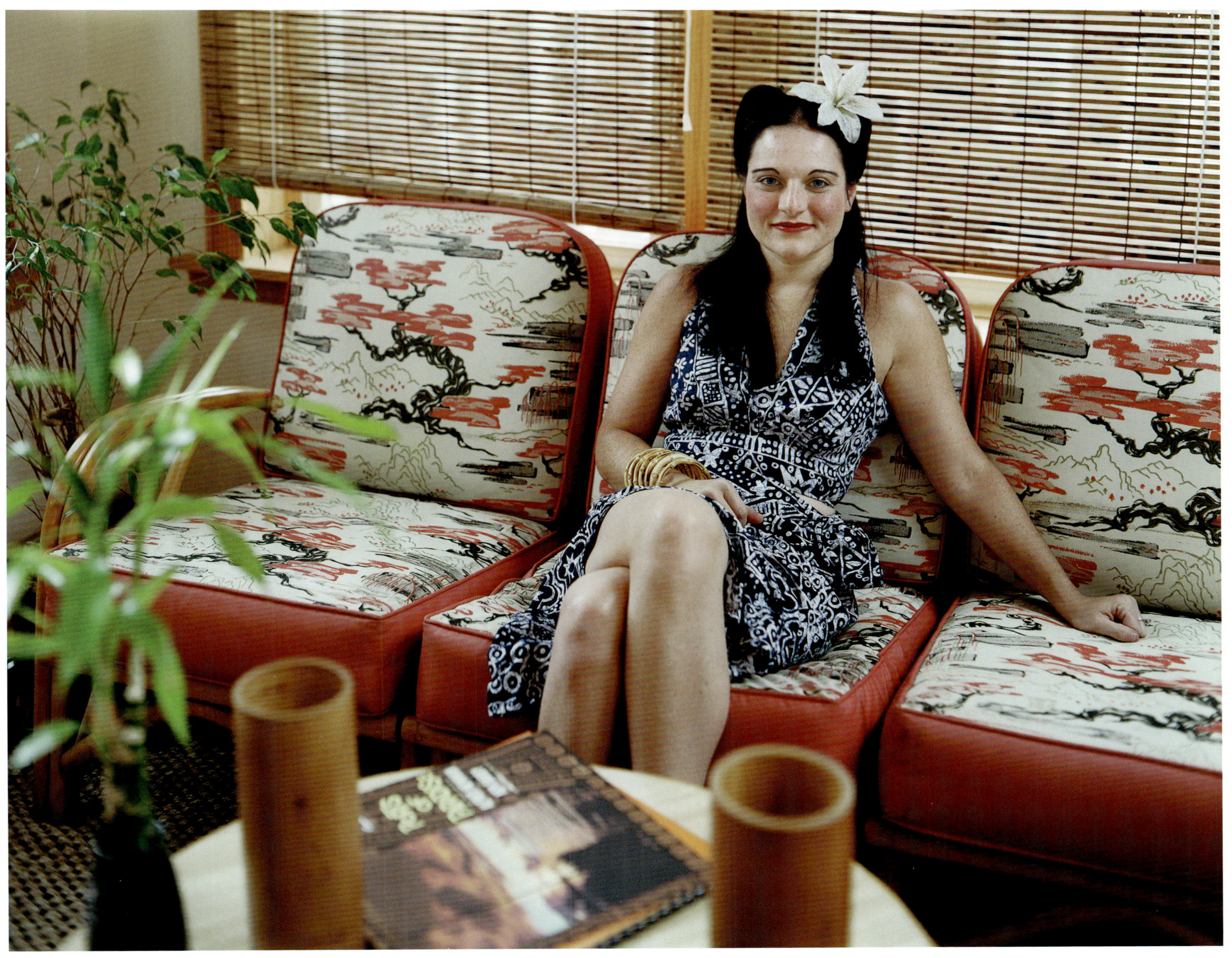

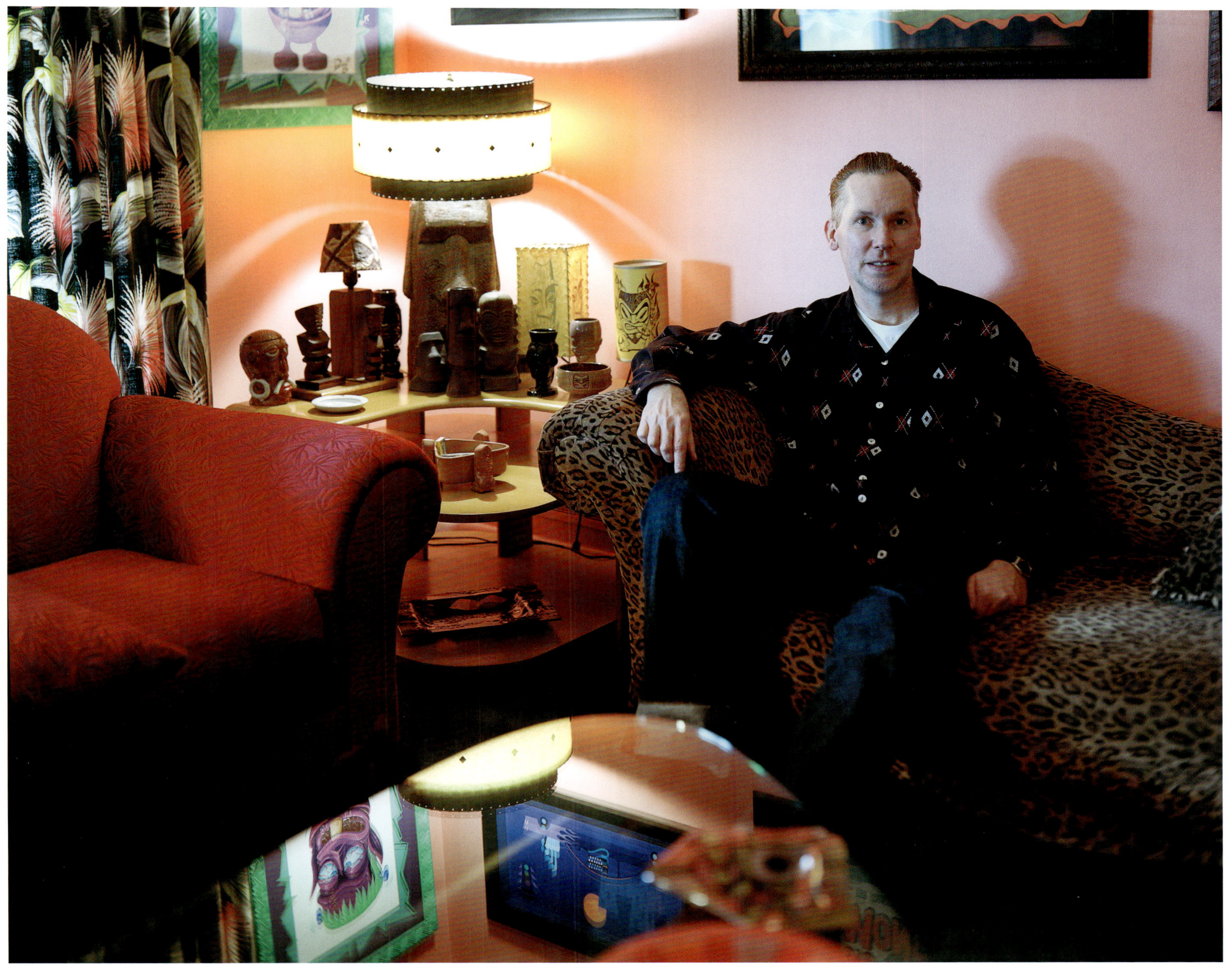

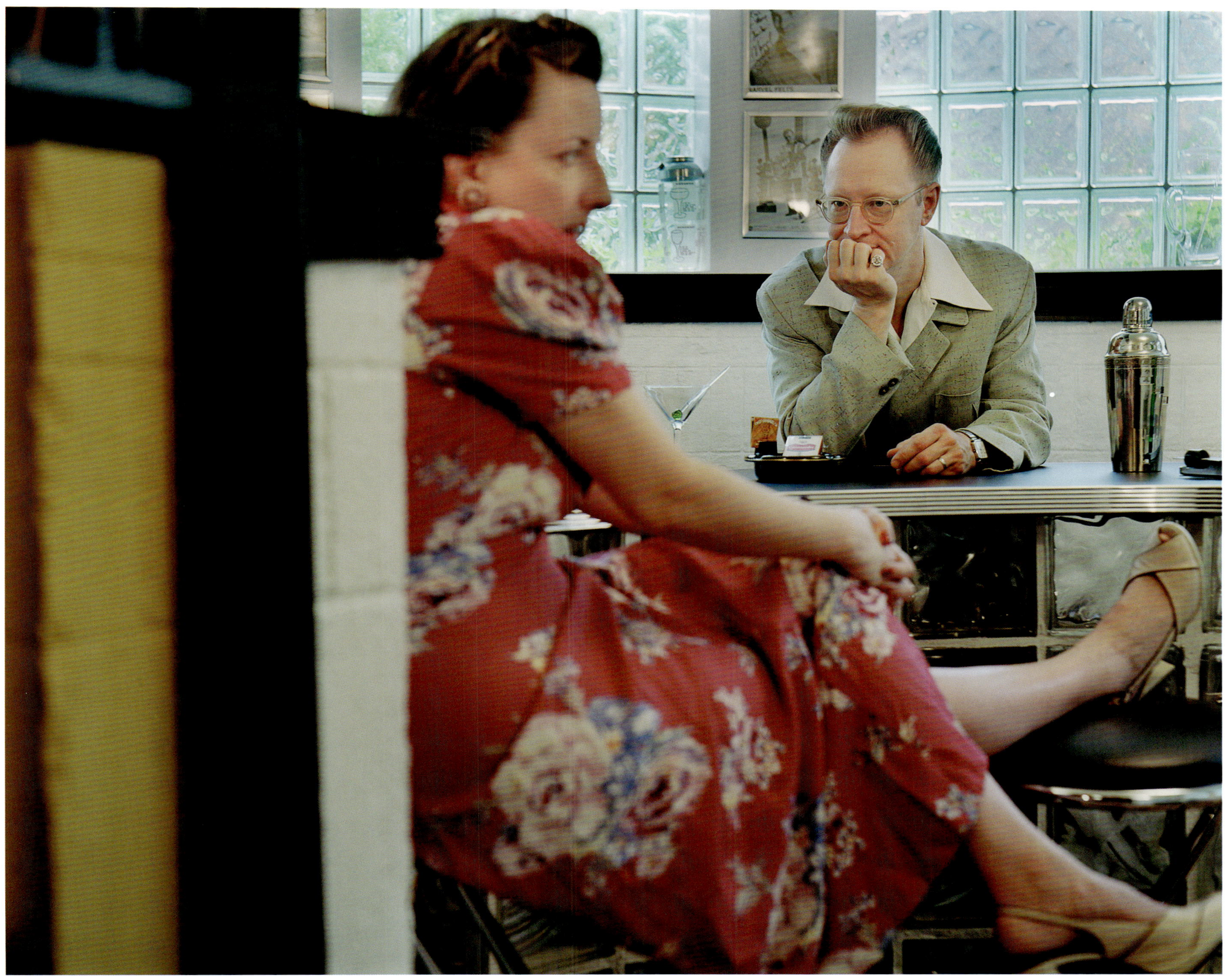

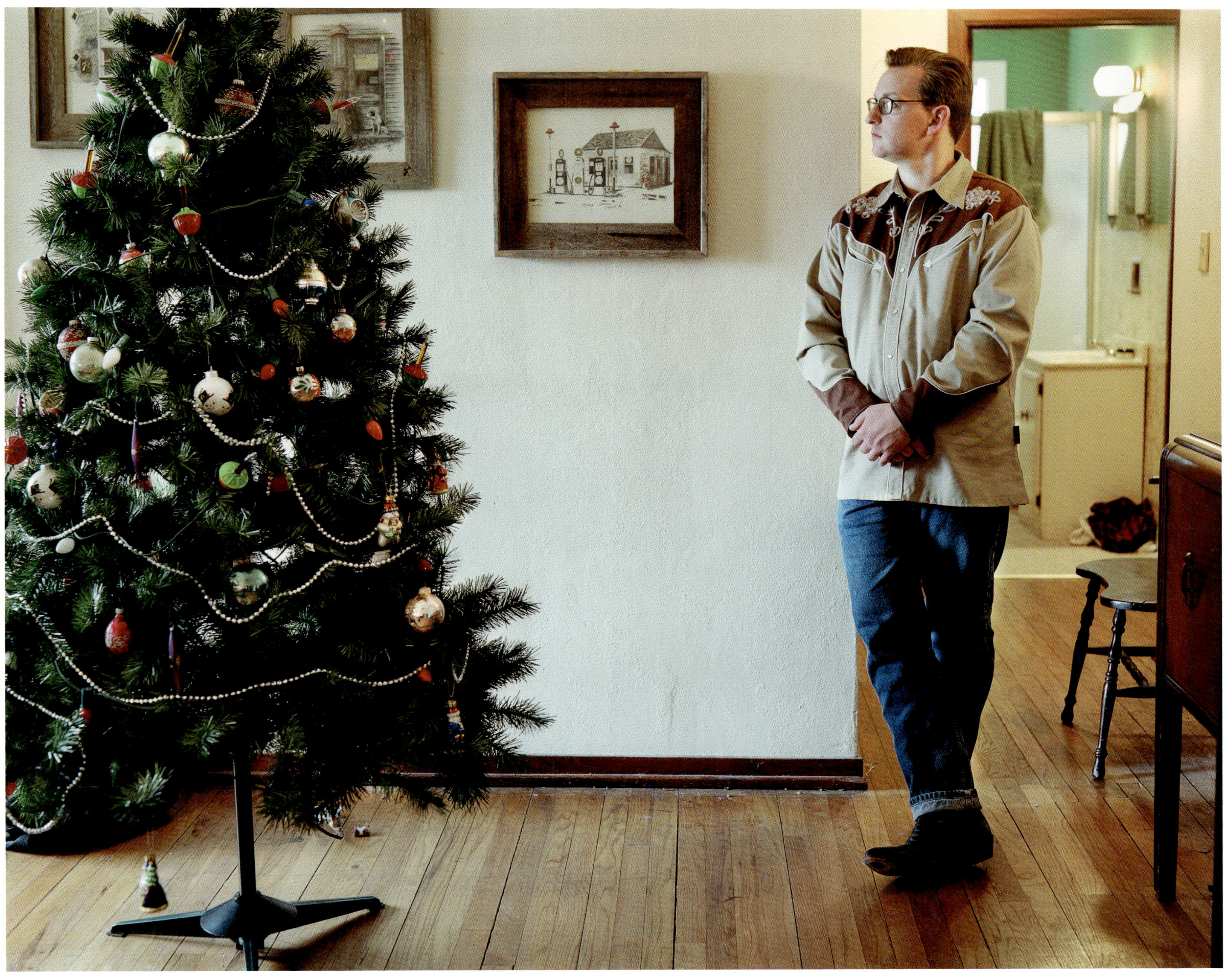

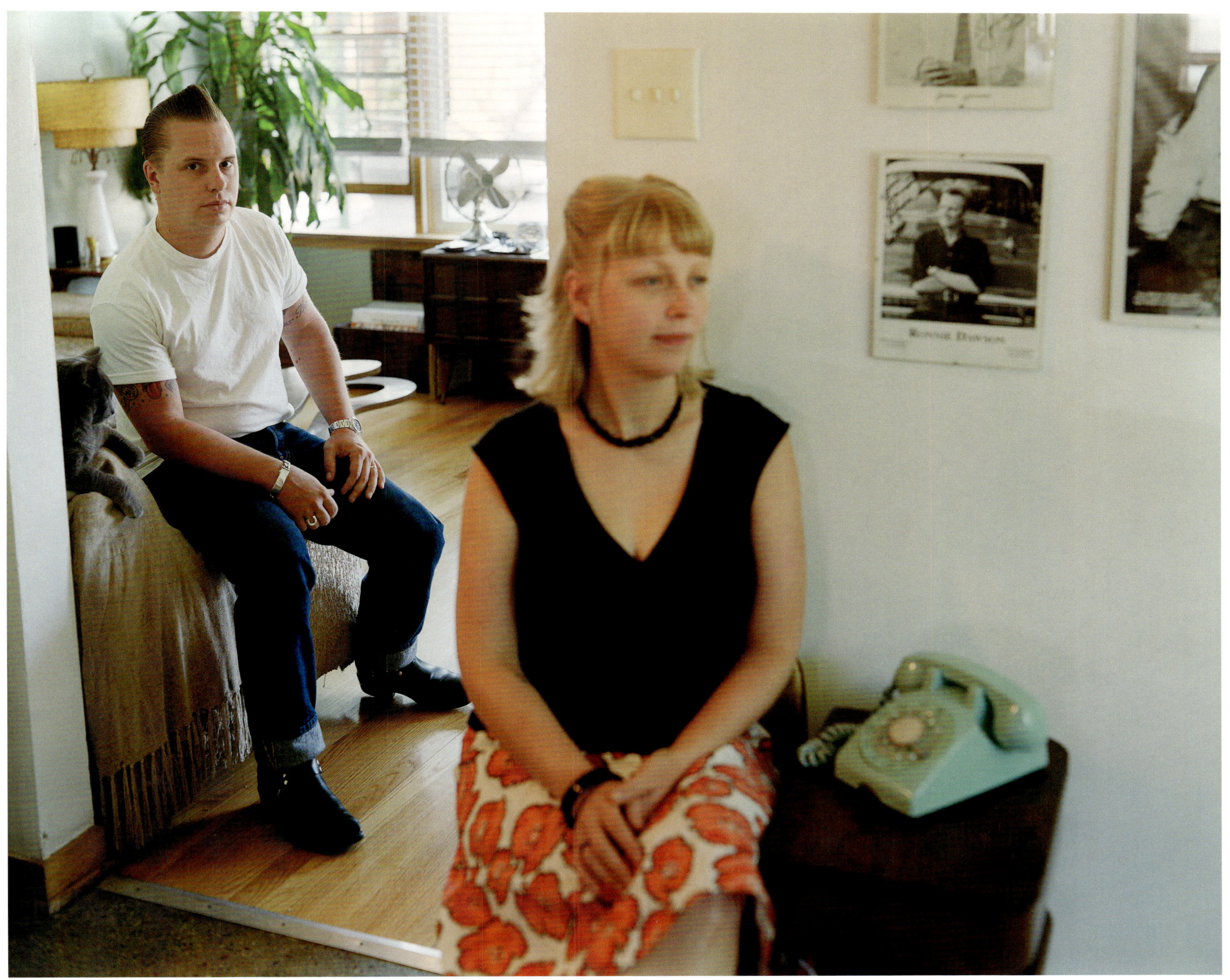

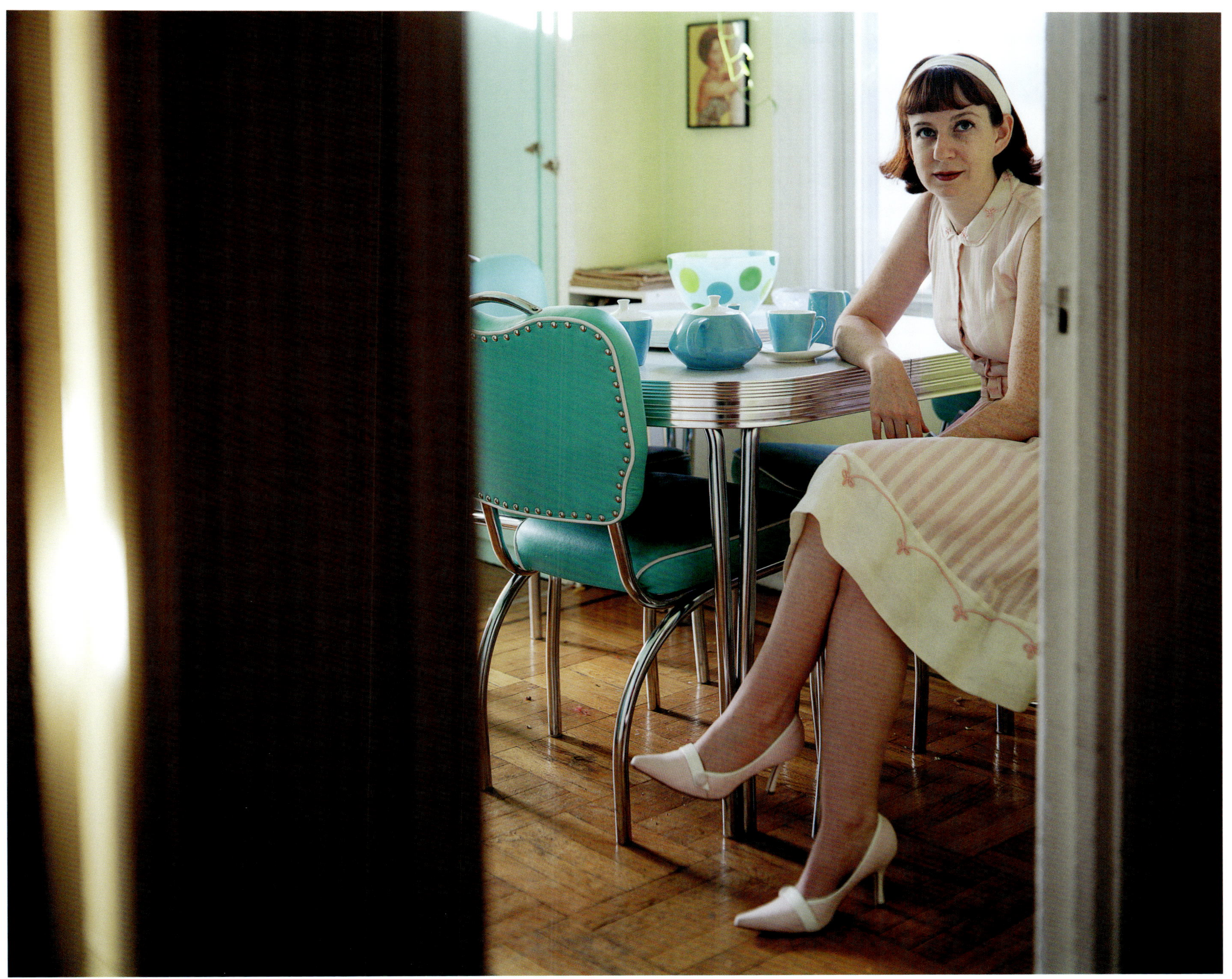

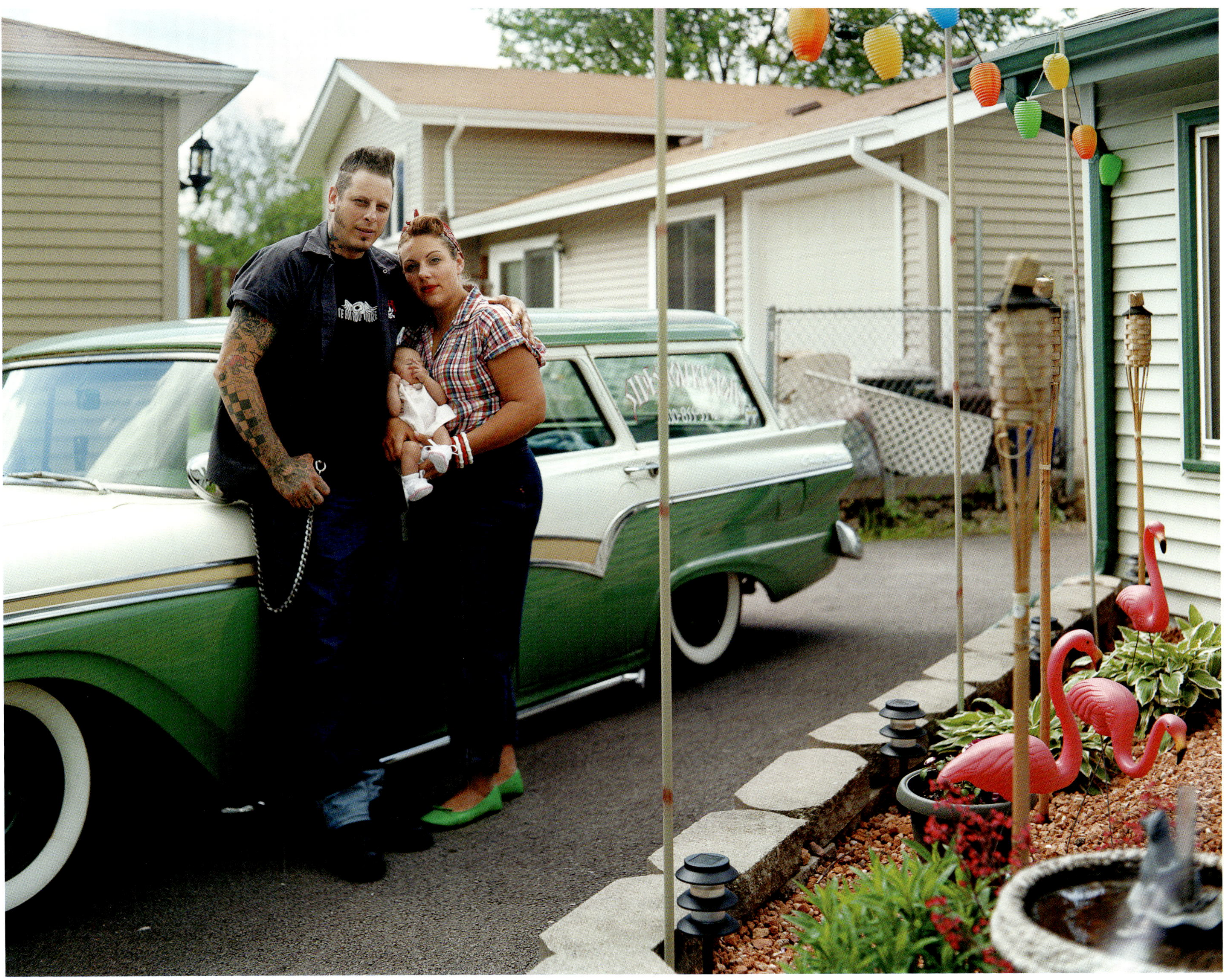

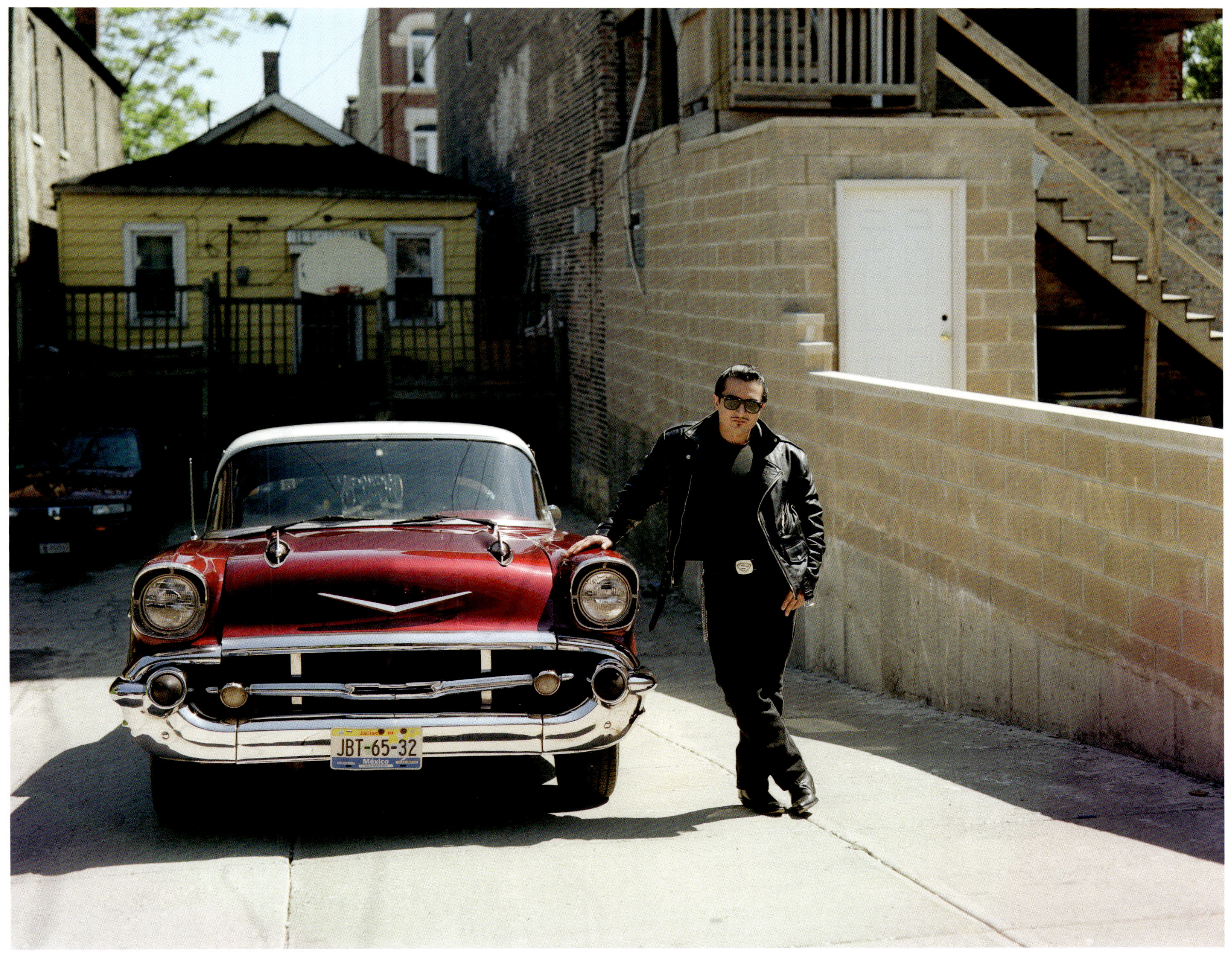

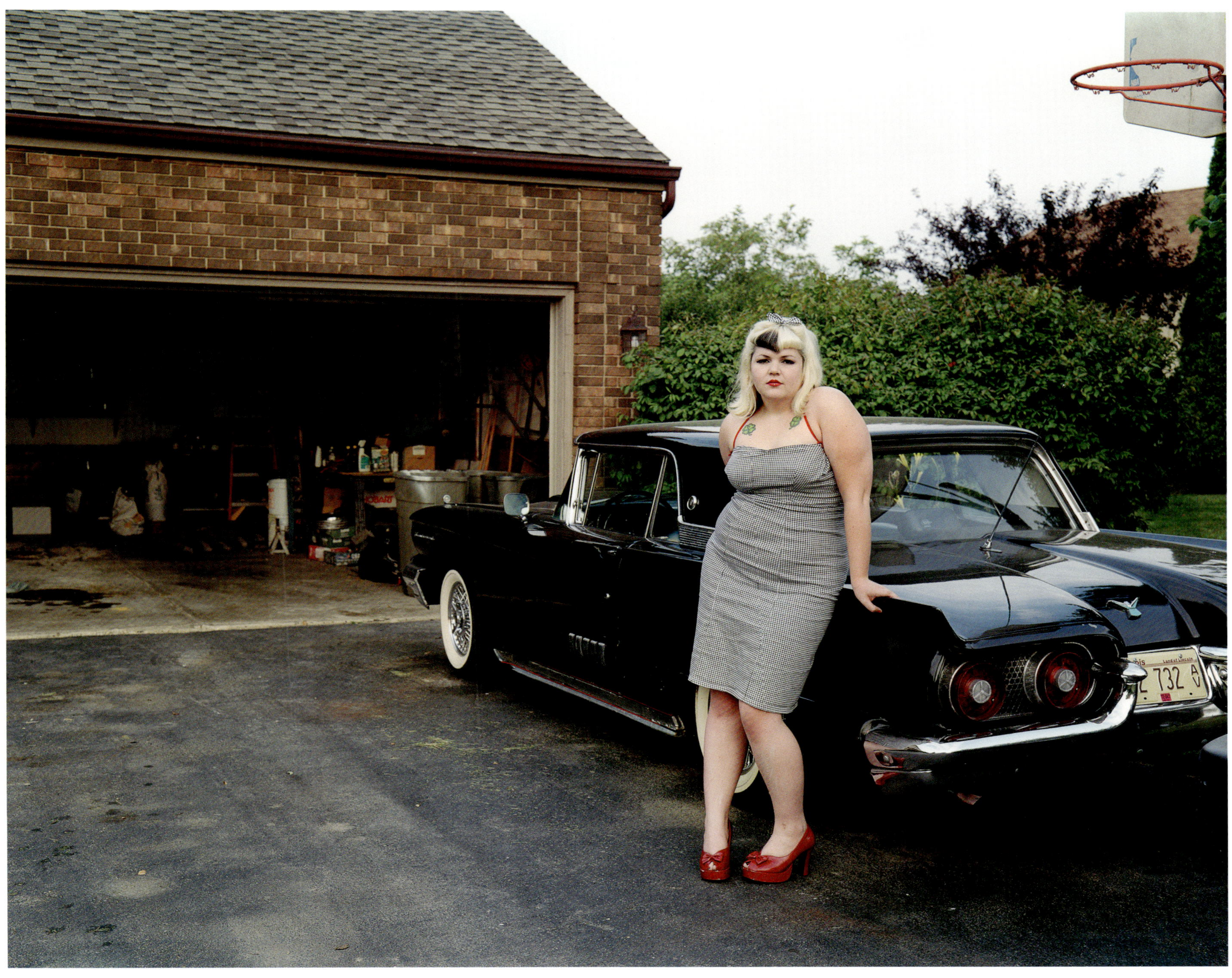

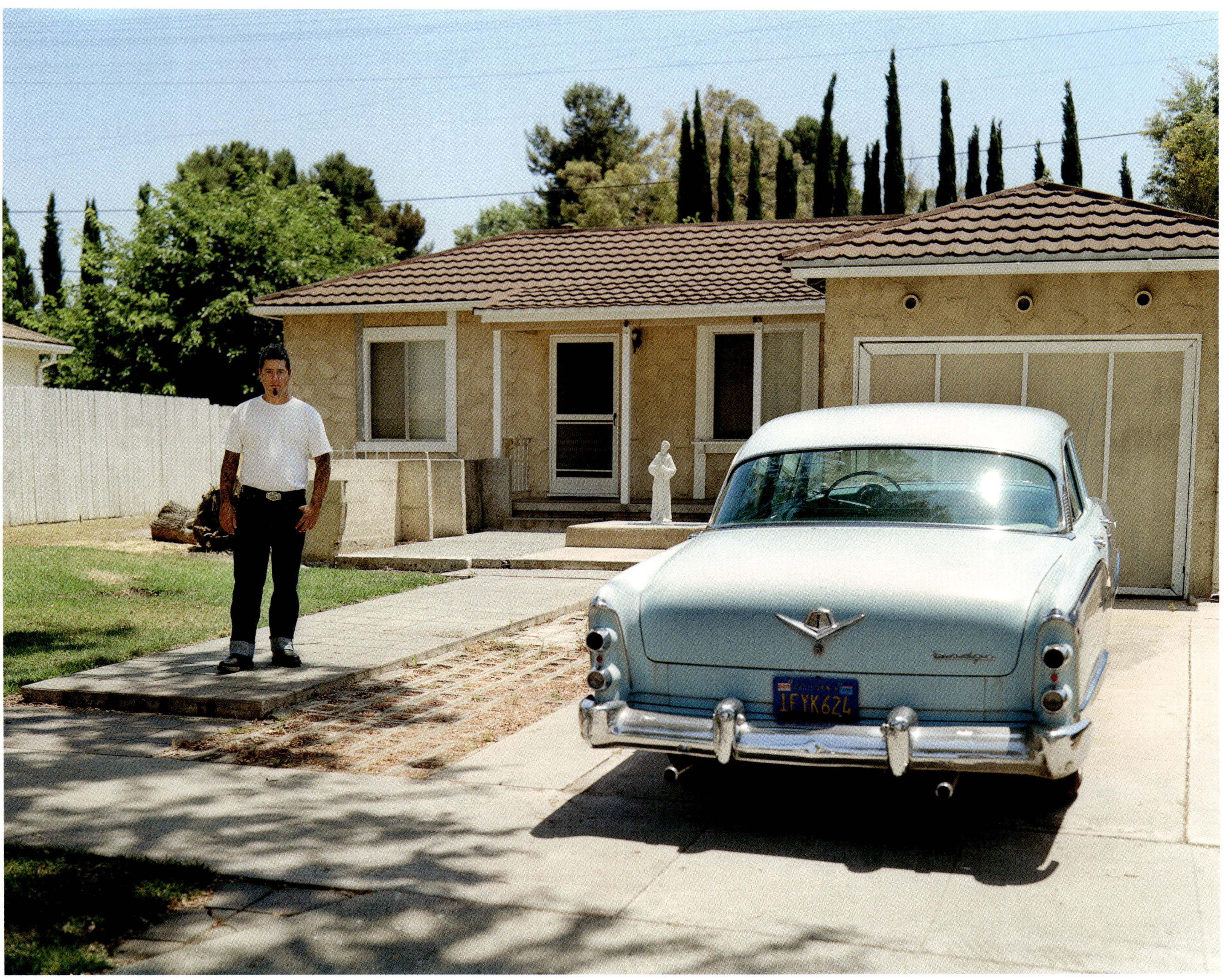

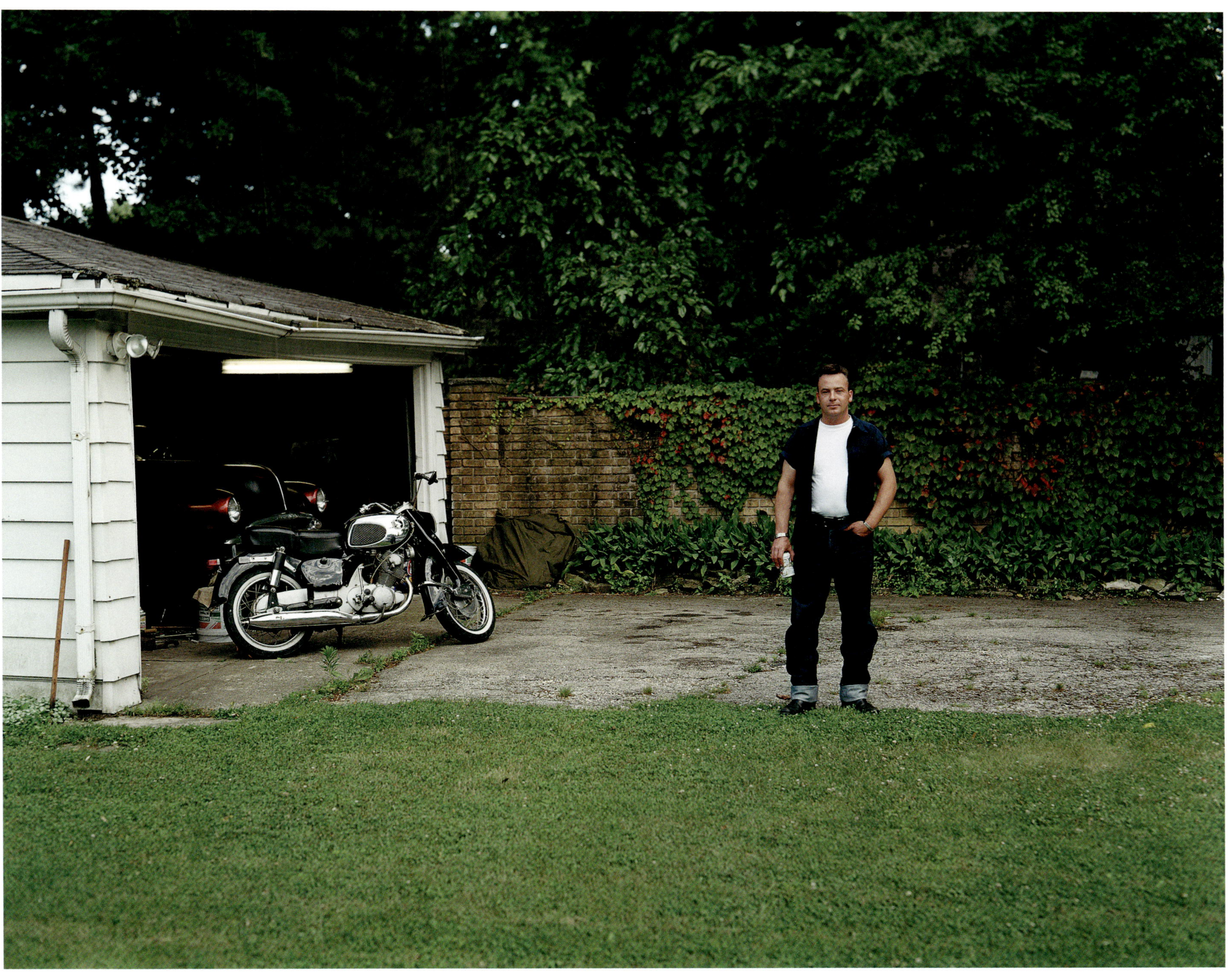

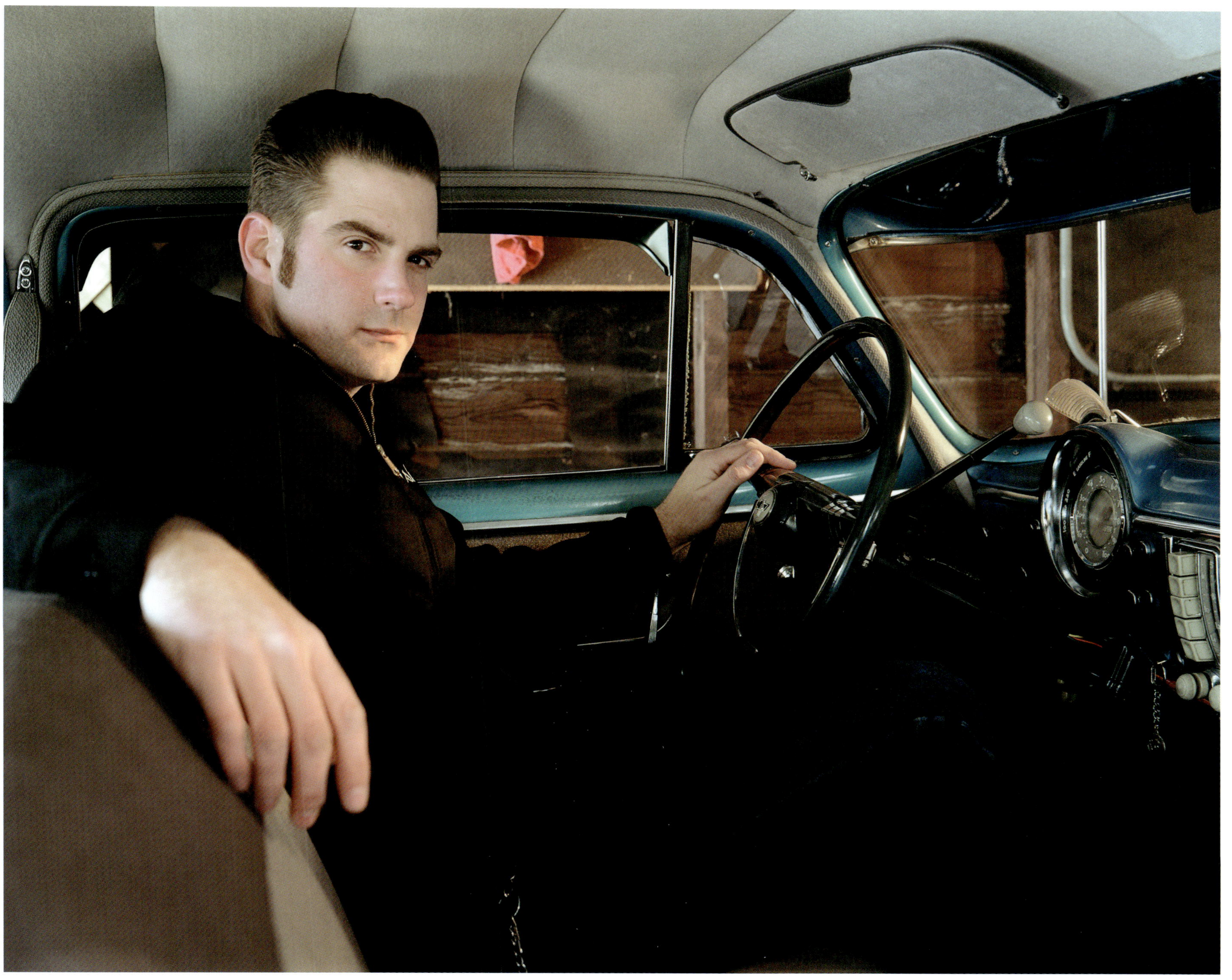

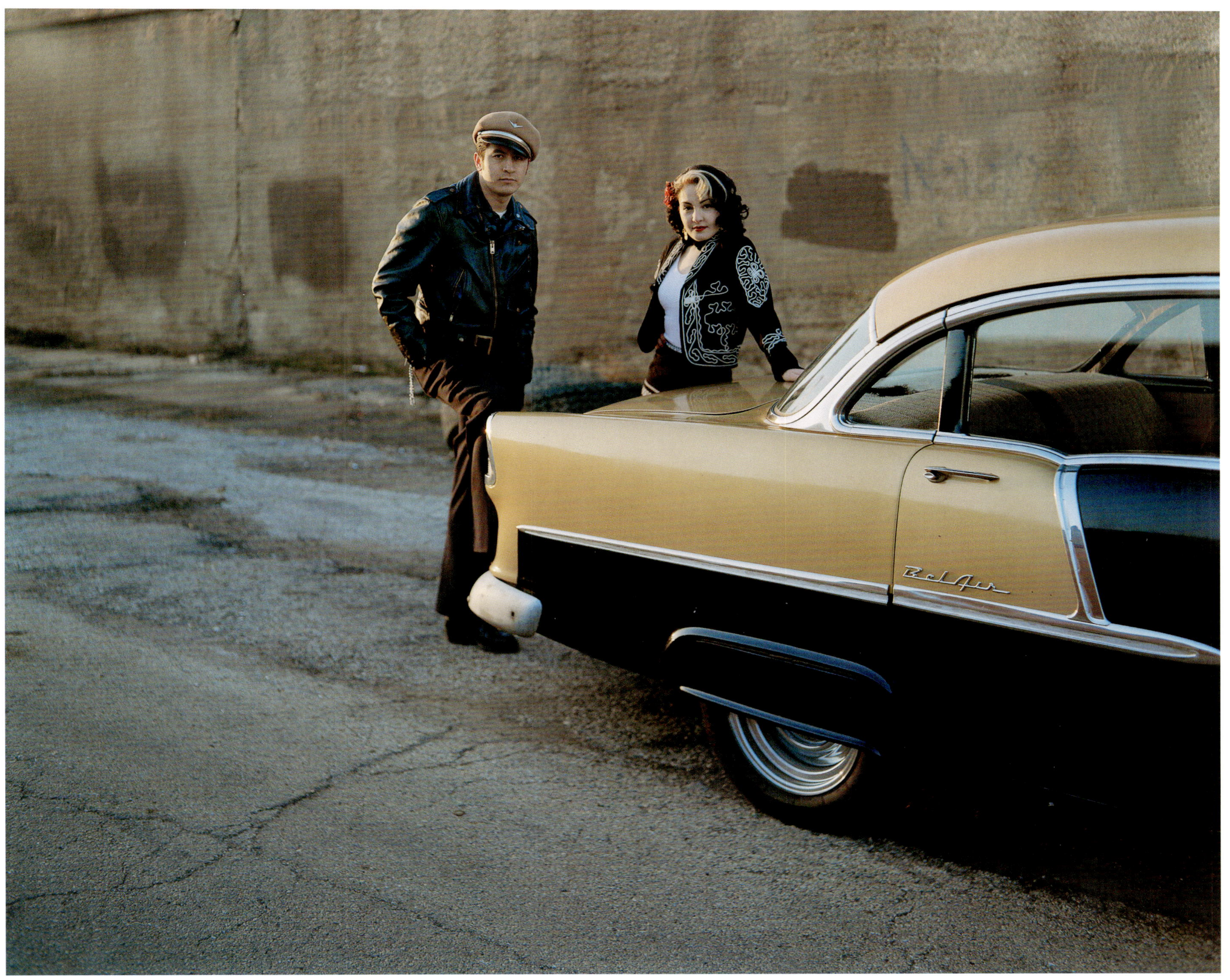

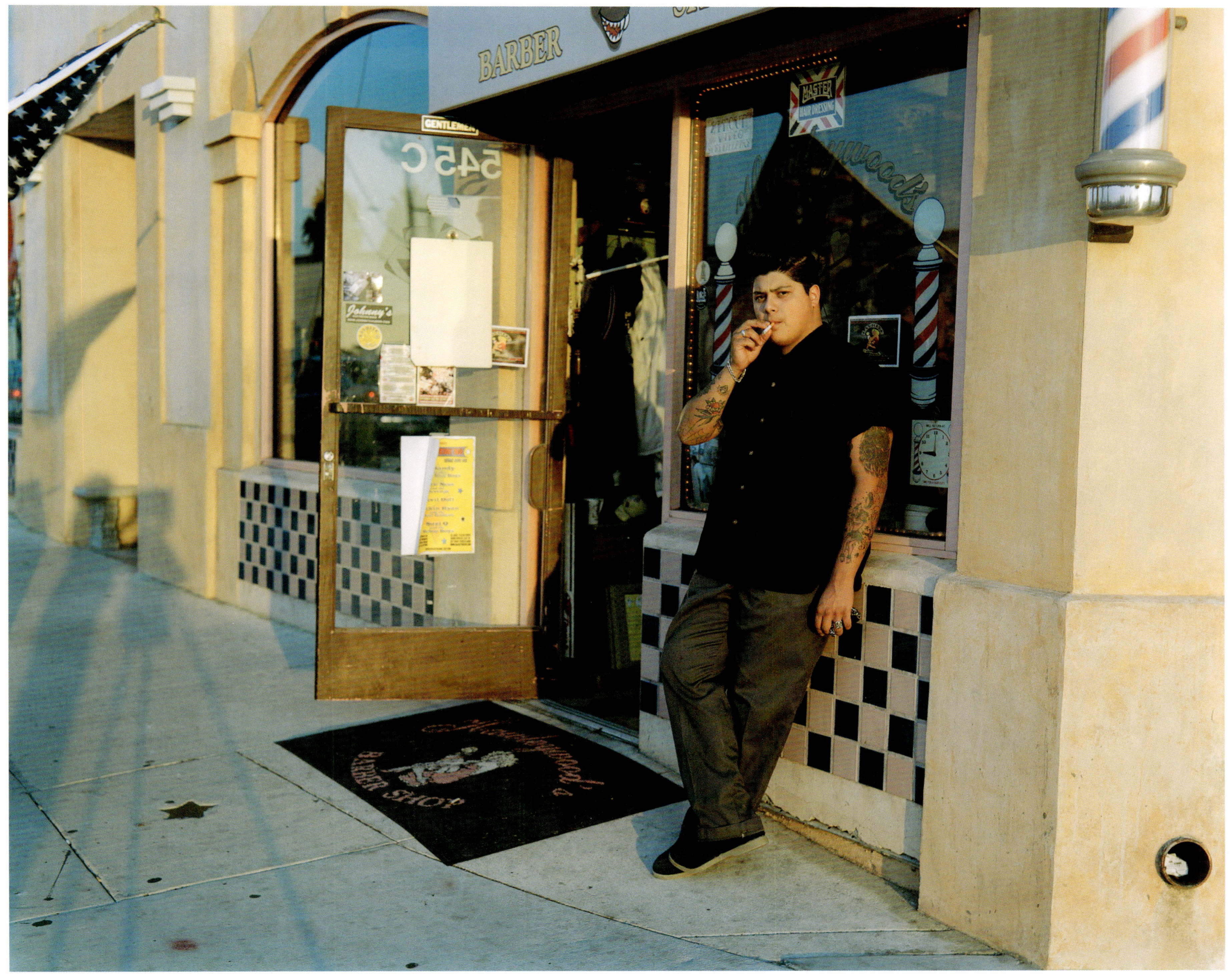

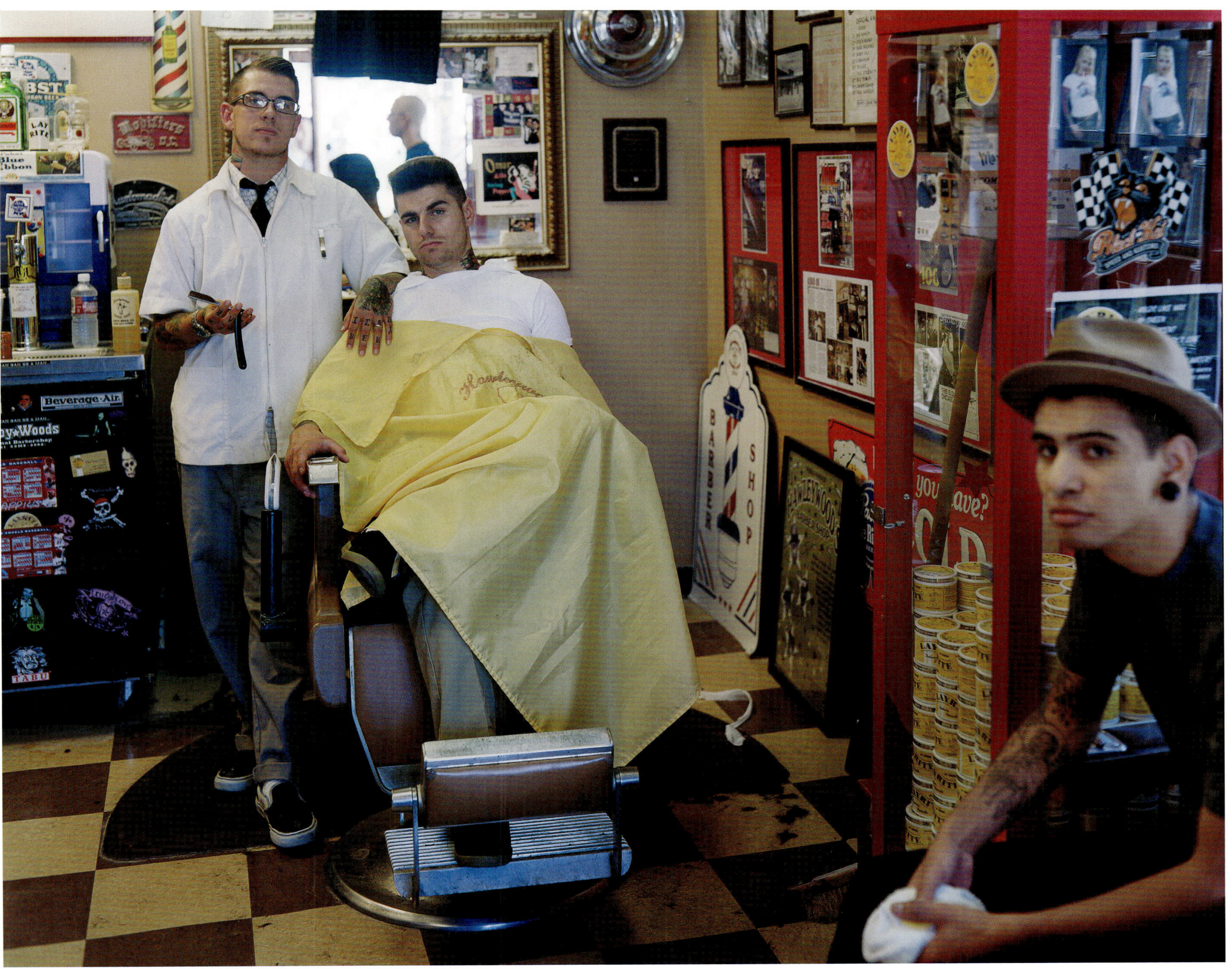

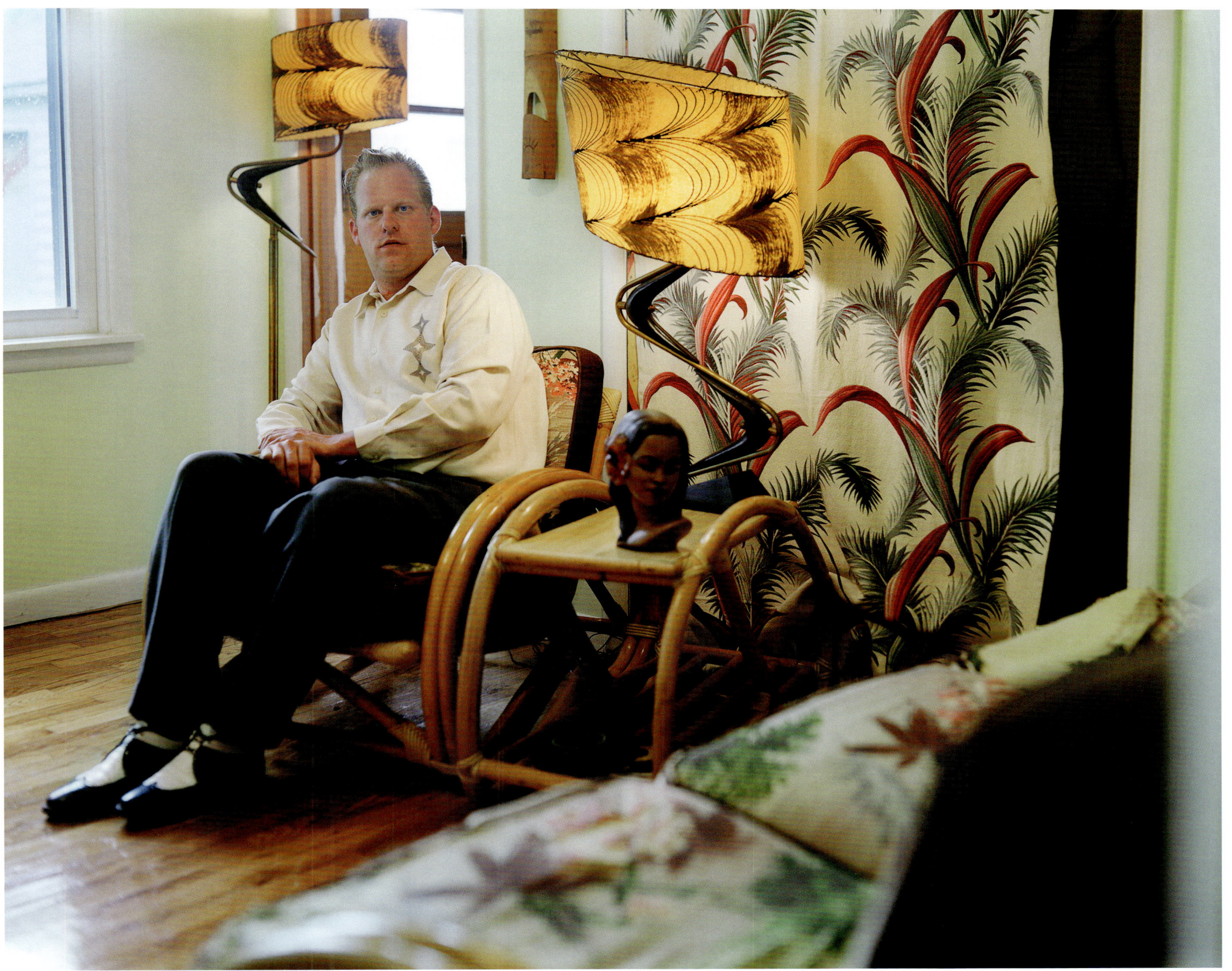

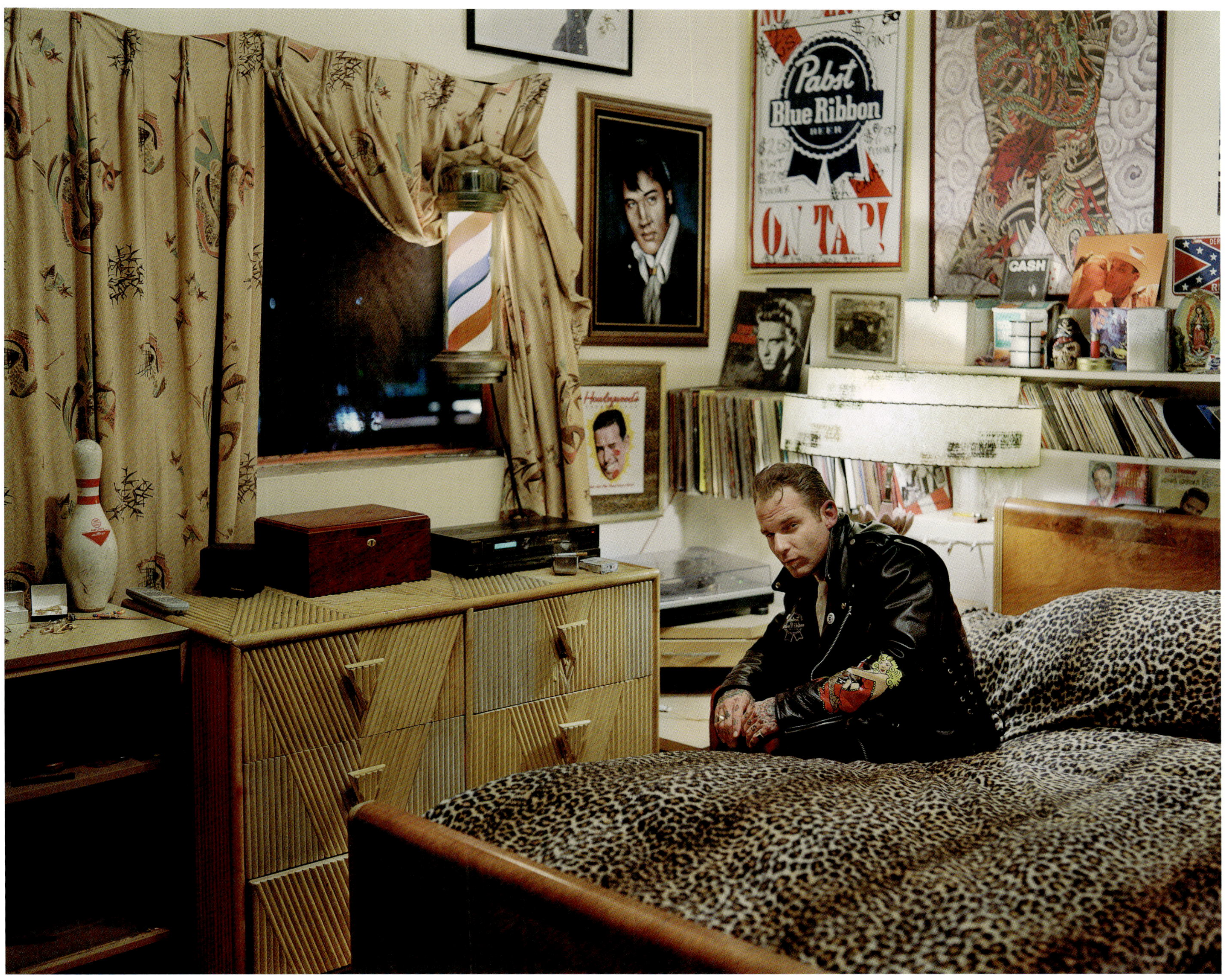

Pabst
Blue Ribbon
BEER
ON TAP!
CASH

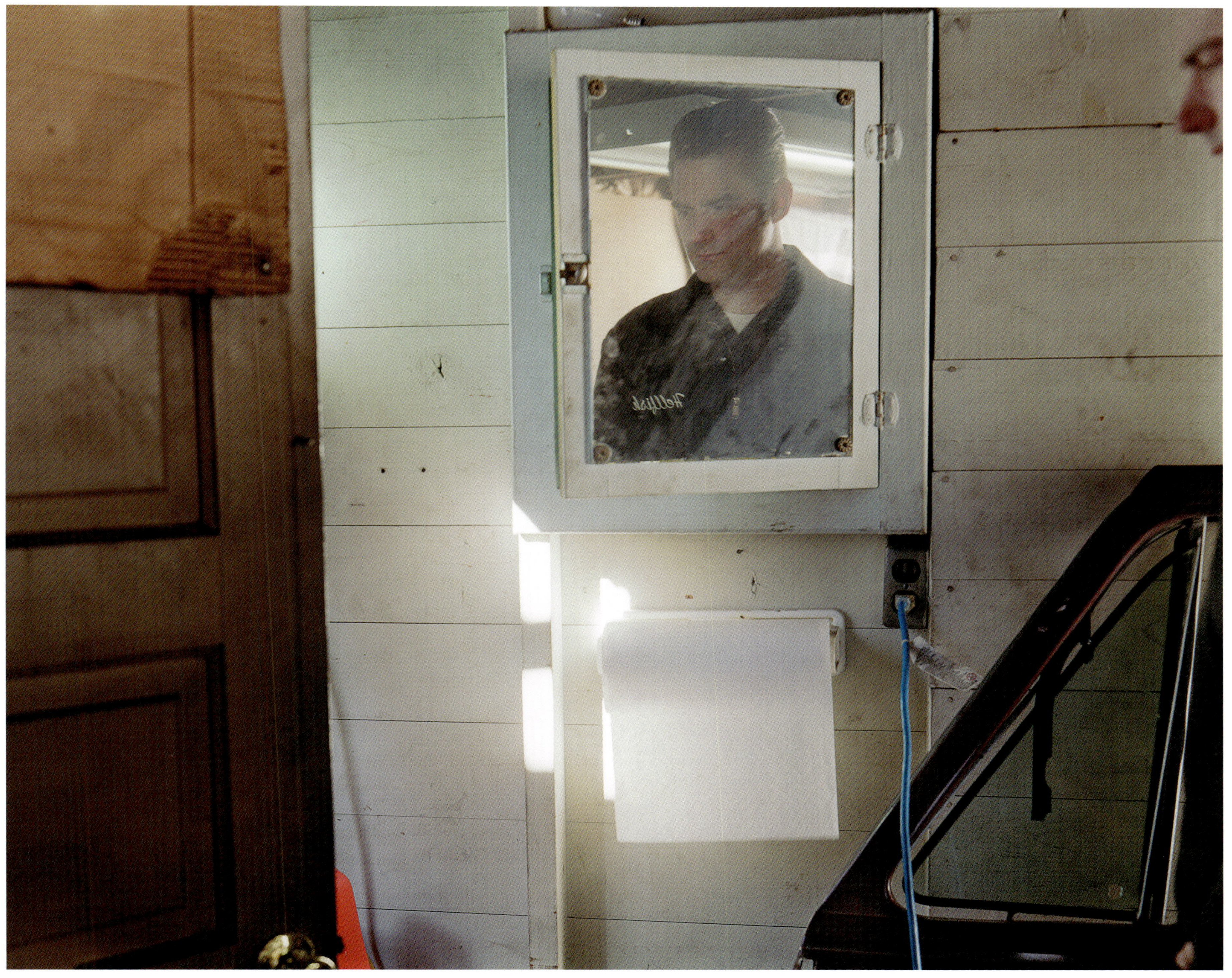

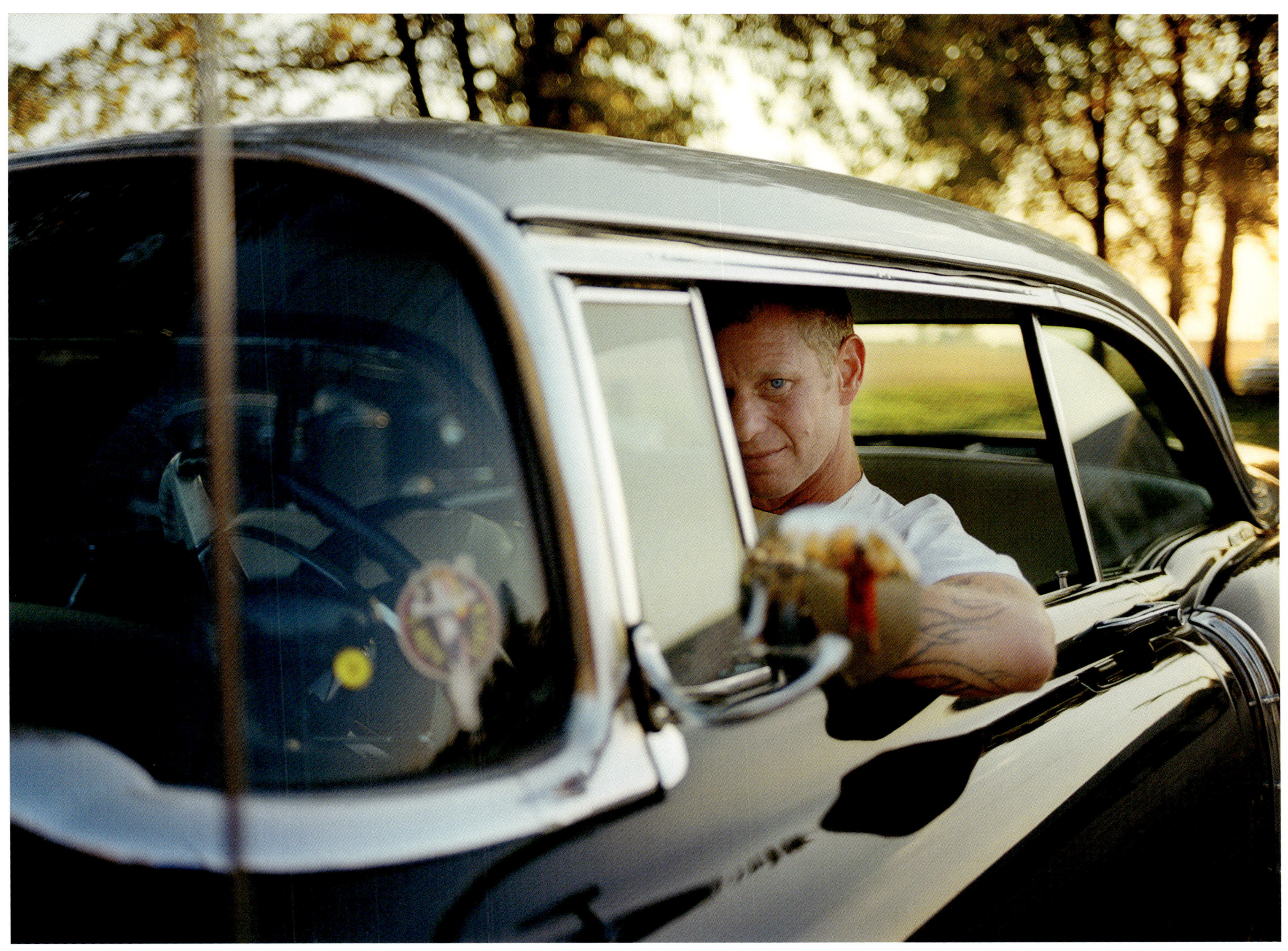

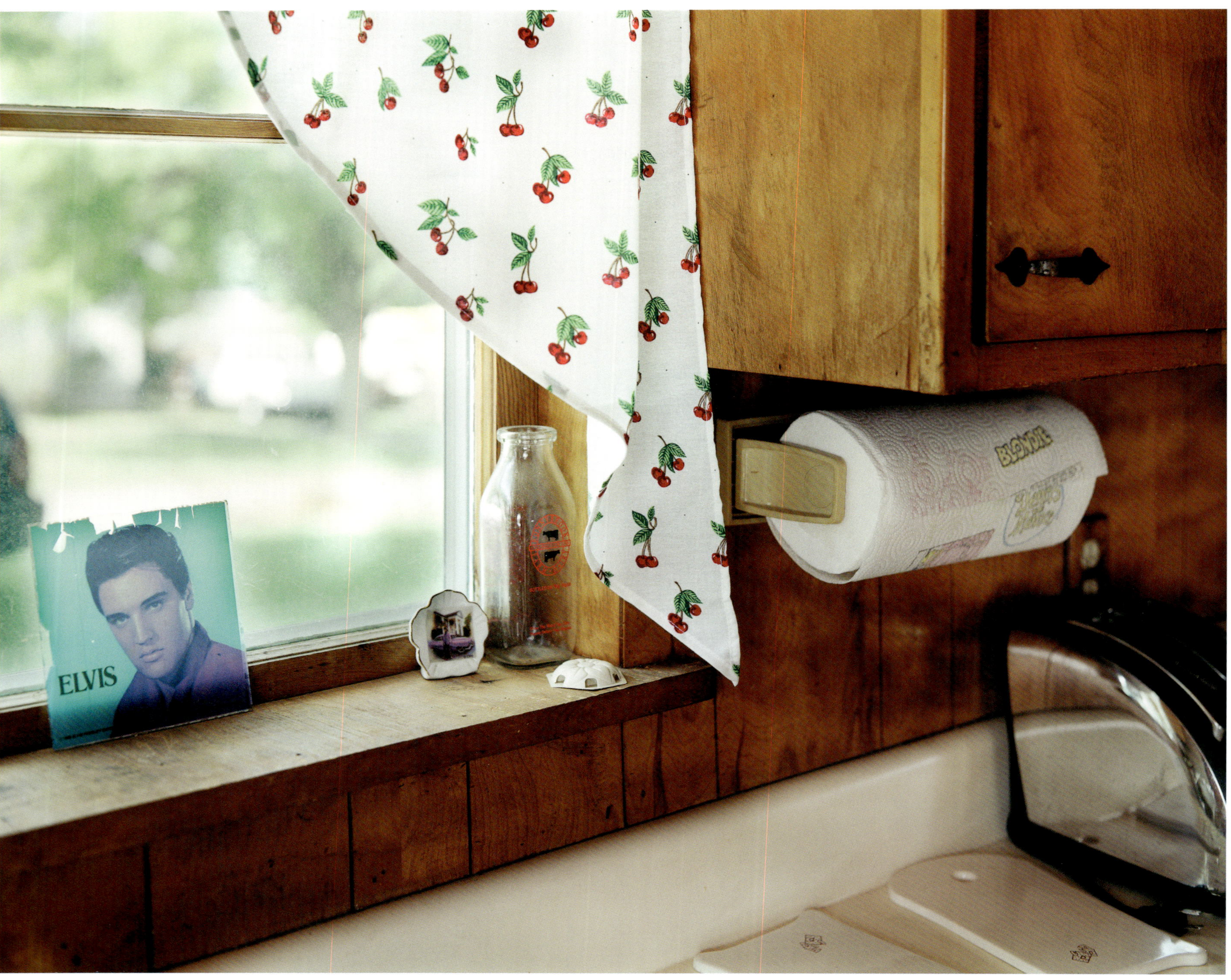

The Rockabillies

by Audrey Michelle Mast

LIKE THE MUSIC THAT INSPIRED IT, rockabilly culture is an amalgam of influences—a contemporary reconfiguration of the texts and images of the 1950s. In her photographs, Jennifer Greenburg both celebrates and critically investigates members a community of people who have built their lives around vintage Americana and mid-century values. They are more than fans or avid collectors: they are passionate, completist, and committed to rockabilly not just as an aesthetic, but as an identity. Greenburg's images capture the visual markers of that identity, the level of that obsession, and the scope of her subjects' commitment to their community and their culture.

When considering *The Rockabillies,* it is helpful first to distinguish between *style* and *fashion* as those terms relate to how we adorn ourselves and our surroundings. In general, *style* is a distinctive form of clothing or designed object. We might also think of style as the distinction, attitude, and flair a person possesses or the overall aesthetic of an era. In contrast, *fashion* connotes ephemerality and transience. As design theorist Malcolm Barnard observes, "while every item of dress may be in a particular style, not every style will be the fashion, as styles go in and out of fashion. And, while every item of dress will be after a certain fashion, not all fashions will be stylish; it is well known that some fashions set out to be anti-style."[1]

Whether we intend to or not, we communicate volumes to others through our appearance. The history of fashion is not just an ebb and flow of rising and falling hemlines, but a set of codes that, when deciphered, help us analyze the cultural mores of a given era or culture. Greenburg allows us to examine these codes in order to scrutinize a past era and our own. Her work encourages us to differentiate between fashion and style and to examine how their differences are used purposefully to communicate a set of ideals.

Many in the rockabilly community discovered the culture of the 1950s through a love of music or vintage design, as Greenburg did. But many discovered it through punk rock—Greenburg notes that "some people call rockabilly the punk rock retirement club"[2] —so it seems odd that so many nonconformists might take up the mantle of the Eisenhower era. Greenburg observes:

> The group appears almost blissfully ignorant of both the realities of the time period so adored and of current realities . . . the imagery and ideals have been taken along with an almost wistful interpretation of the time . . . taken out of context from the reality of a time period that saw race riots, great hardship, and little hope for middle-class advancement . . ..[3]

In spite of its escapist leanings, one might argue that this brand of fifties revivalism is as radical as punk in its rejection of contemporary norms. Rockabilly shares punk's DIY (do-it-yourself) ethos and love of unbridled rock and roll, but it is not an anti-establishment movement. The rockabillies' conservativism is neither overtly political nor confrontational. It is oriented inward, toward the making of community, and there is a distinct lack of the self-destructive tendencies exhibited by many youth-oriented subcultures, like punk. Unlike conservative movements in America, however, which are typically based upon religious belief, rockabilly does not hold a shared ideology at its core nor is it foisted on society at large. Rockabilly is, in fact, quite insular and can be best understood as a kind of quiet rebellion—a subculture but not a counterculture. It is a personal insurgence against the threat of the new and a support network based precisely on that shared threat. It is a pastiche of ideals—a sanguine interpretation of fifties life culled from its iconography and its perceived simplicity. Rockabilly is not about nostalgia in the literal sense: Greenburg's subjects are not pining for a bygone era in the way that someone might wish to relive their youth. Since most were born long after the fifties they are not reliving history but are, instead, selectively choosing the art and artifacts of that era they wish to celebrate and consciously overlooking the rest. Greenburg's images are simulacra of the fifties: they are neither a likeness to nor a copy of historical reality, but they do, as Baudrillard might say, create their own truth.

The idea of rockabilly as pastiche extends not only to the community's selective idolatry of the fifties, but to the sheer breadth of subcultural influences that affect the rockabilly scene. Much of its style is drawn from several decidedly non-mainstream facets of the fifties: burlesque, pin-up photography, and hot-rod culture. Another key influence is the tastes of what was then an emergent demographic asserting itself for the first time: teenagers. Music historian Craig Morrison writes, "rockabilly's first practitioners were young, mostly in their teens and early twenties, an age group affected by the postwar rise in urbanization and affluence of the working class. They were part of an emerging 'consumption-oriented youth subculture centered around automobiles, fast food, movies, and especially, radio and recordings.'"[4] The emerging youth-oriented consumerism of yesteryear is today's booming antiques market. Acquiring vintage clothing, housewares, and memorabilia or restoring a vintage home or car can be an expensive pursuit, but their choices as consumers are limited; for most Americans, in contrast, there is the constant specter of something newer, faster, and better. So often nostalgia is entwined with kitsch (particularly in regard to the post-World War II era), but the rockabillies place a premium on authenticity. They may be sentimental, but they are not superficial; their fixation on fifties style is not merely a fleeting participation in its fashion.

Though we cannot assume that all members of the community live blithely unaware of the customs of a less progressive era, immersion in this world has strong incentives for both men and women: a strong sense of belonging, in particular. The tight-knit network of rockabillies across the nation and even abroad is a postmodern tribe, bound together by a devotional fervor to their lifestyle, a set of shared values, and a common aesthetic. French sociologist Michel Maffesoli first identified the emergence of such "affectual" tribes (participatory, organic communities that replace the hierarchies of institutions like corporations and churches) in 1988, but the Internet has increased the scope and intensity of these associations. Rockabillies may be neo-Luddites in many respects, but they have utilized social networking to strengthen their fiercely loyal local groups into a nationwide community. No matter how far they travel, they are drawn to one another. "We trust each other before we have ever met," says Greenburg, of encountering other members of the rockabilly culture who are easily identified by their appearances.[5] Both men and women use style as an immediate, visceral, and instantly recognizable signifier of their membership in the group.

After the economic and political upheavals of the thirties and forties, as the post-war era saw a return to traditional gender roles and an emphasis on the nuclear family, fashion became more profoundly gendered. Today, although both men and women in the rockabilly community pay close attention to their look, it can be argued that each gender experiences differently their stylistic choices.

Men's dress since the fifties, and its meaning, has not changed as profoundly as female dress has. Art historian Anne Hollander notes that the male suit evolved approximately a century ago and hasn't changed much since. She writes that "men's clothes clearly do not participate in fashion, since 'men's fashion' is an acknowledged subset and has scarcely any of the fame and relevance attaching to 'fashion.'"[6] This is not to say that rockabilly men are making contemporary choices. Pompadour hairstyles and brothel creeper shoes, for example, are clear markers of an older look. But the cuffed jeans, white tees, open-collared shirts, fedoras, and leather jackets worn by Greenburg's male subjects do not necessarily read as overtly eccentric or "retro." If anything, their look tends to evoke notions of "classic" men's fashion, and many men today might simply regard an accessory like a fedora as a mark of sophistication, a signifier of a time when "men were men." This is the appeal of the strong gender divide in both fifties style generally and rockabilly style specifically.

Women's fashion of the same era is exaggeratedly feminine. The fifties standard of beauty—an hourglass figure enhanced by a wasp-waisted silhouette and polished, carefully coiffed grooming—is still considered to be the archetypical feminine look. It is the last era of what is now known as "Hollywood glamour." The antiquated meaning of *glamour* is a magical spell or charm—an illusion cast by witches. Glamour, then, is not pure beauty but a sort of stagecraft, an allure or illusion aided by clothes, cosmetics, and hair or, as in the case of an object like a car, a streamlined, sensual, and flashy design. Fashion historian Virginia Postrel writes, "glamour is not just beauty or luxury. It is not a style but an effect, a quality that depends on the play of imagination. Its power is not sensation but inspiration. Glamour is never boring . . . it is, to quote a recent fashion blurb, about 'transcending the everyday.'"[7]

In difficult economic times, particularly among Greenburg's young subjects, the rockabilly lifestyle offers a way of transcending the everyday. They utilize style and create glamour without being consumers of fashion, with all its seasonal whims, high prices, and inaccessibility to those who have a less-than-ideal body type. It can also be, or at least it might once have been, a source of subversive power. Cultural critic Penny Sparke, tracing the evolution of "feminine taste" from its roots in the Victorian era to its permutations in contemporary life, notes that, during the post-war era, modern fashions "enhanced gender differences at a time when the roles of men and women were highly polarized," but identified "the impracticality of the stiletto heel and the full skirts acting of open resistance" in their rejection of utilitarian, wartime garb.[8] For those who see today's fashion as increasingly too casual or gauche, reclaiming fifties-era style is a similar act of defiance.

One might argue that rockabillies, particularly the women, are not always choosing a simpler life (whether or not the fifties ever were truly "simpler" than today is arguable). Their look, both in their homes and in their personal appearance, takes an enormous amount of effort and attention to detail—a level of care to which many contemporary women would never commit. They're choosing a more glamorous life, and creating a personal style, an environment, and an existence touched with a sort of self-made magic. The ritual of dressing and primping at a vanity, for instance—evoked in *Jolie in Her Bedroom* on page 13 and *Mrs. Smith missing Chuck* on page 15—epitomizes this quixotic approach to everyday life. As rigid as their gender roles might be, women in the rockabilly scene are able and, moreover, *expected* to accentuate their femininity, albeit within an existing framework. Some women have found it oppressive, such as New Wave musician-turned rockabilly revivalist Pearl Harbour, who has observed that "the only way for a girl to hold her own in rockabilly culture is to look good all the time."[9] But, for most, classic glamour itself is an enjoyable subversion of contemporary norms through a commitment to a style that is no longer in fashion.

When addressing her own place in rockabilly culture, Greenburg describes herself as "both a participant and voyeur."[10] She is both a knowledgeable insider and an outsider (particularly in her politics and her academic background). Her entrée into the insular rockabilly community happened gradually over a number of years, while she slowly gained the trust of the people she has photographed. The images reflect the photographer's history within the community, both in their tender consideration of her subjects and the sheer improbability of capturing them otherwise. Greenburg has no interest in depicting her subjects as "the other," exoticizing what viewers might perceive as eccentricities. Formally, their poses tend to evoke the same mid-century feature magazine photography that is the rockabillies' source material, but Greenburg's compositions, which include deep-focus detail on the outskirts of the images, are much more contemporary. Underneath the surface of Greenburg's saturated celebration of rockabilly culture are deeper conceptual underpinnings. The photos capture an authentic likeness of contemporary rockabillies' lives, but they are not conceived as documentary and do not function in that way. She has said that her subjects are "interested in their own iconography," and she chooses to show them as just that—icons. For Greenburg, "candid photography would be a betrayal of [her subjects] inherent value system," and, as a photographer and member of the community, she is "dedicated to preserving their pathos."[11]

Greenburg's interaction with her subjects during a shoot is extremely unobtrusive and, to a great degree, collaborative. Her process is also intimate: using a manual, 4 x 5 view camera that forces her to face her subjects directly, there is no "hiding behind the lens." It is a slow, methodical process. Mounted on a tripod, the camera is static, mirroring the subjects' wish to remain stationary in their way of life. Greenburg's method allows them to self-direct the way they wish to appear; she asks them to choose their location and their pose. As Susan Sontag has observed, the act of posing can be inherently awkward. In an analysis of Diane Arbus's pictures of eccentric characters on the streets of New York City, she notes that Arbus's subjects are encouraged to pose rather than to act natural. Sontag notes that "standing or sitting stiffly makes them *seem like images of themselves*."[12] Though Greenburg neither views her subjects with the detached curiosity of Arbus nor encourages an intentional awkwardness, a similar effect is present in her work. Her subjects pose to compound their glamour; that is to say, her treatment of them as "icons" lends them a sort of hyperreality. They are "images of themselves," much in the same way we might experience a photograph of Marilyn Monroe not as the document of a person but as the image of an icon.

Greenburg's technical and conceptual pedigree is noteworthy in this regard: she learned to use the 4 x 5 view camera from legendary photographer Kenneth Josephson at the School of the Art Institute of Chicago. "Ken gave me a sense of adventure," she says.[13] Later, she studied with Laura Letinsky at the University of Chicago, who is, perhaps, best known for lush photographic still lifes that depict the aftermath of (staged, nonexistent) debaucherous dinner parties—austere but intricate evocations of classical painting. Letinsky encouraged Greenburg to experiment and find the art in her photography practice.[14] Greenburg shares Letinsky's ability to make minute detail seem extremely significant, even talismanic; our eyes are drawn to the rich subtleties of each image. In *Stuart's kitchen* on page 74, one of Greenburg's rare images in which a human figure is not present, we see a simple but loaded tableau: a cheerful cherry-print curtain, a chrome toaster, a translucent Elvis Presley image on glass, and a milk bottle. But closer examination reveals another object that seems almost preposterous in its specificity and rarity: a roll of "Blondie" comic paper towels. It speaks volumes about Stuart's talent for authentic minutiae as well as Greenburg's attention to its implications.

Upon first glance, the photographic sequence of *The Rockabillies* seems like an elaborate, stage-set period piece. As with discovering the paper towels in *Stuart's kitchen,* a close examination of Greenburg's images reveals small incongruities in the fifties aura of her subjects. We see a videocassette recorder, a neighbor's contemporary car, and a modern-looking extension cord. These components of the images are a sort of *punctum,* which Roland Barthes describes as "that accident which pricks me (but also bruises me, is poignant to me)."[15] Years later, Hal Foster described the punctum of Warhol's disaster series as being its sheer repetition, particularly the slippage of registration of the silkscreen. This imperfection, he argues, is what "allows the real to poke through."[16] In a Greenburg image, the "slippage" of modern life into such picturesque, old-fashioned imagery is what reminds us of the reality and intricacy of its post-millennial creation.

Several of Greenburg's subjects, however, are pierced or visibly tattooed, though often in a retro-inspired style. In these images, we are more keenly aware that the subject is contemporary, and there is no subtle punctum. The focal point of the image is, instead, the frisson between the old and new, the seemingly incongruous juxtaposition of prominent tattoos on a woman whose appearance is, in all other respects, in accordance with the arch-feminine ideal, as in *Lucy-Jane in her signature color* on page 7). Even images in which virtually no indication of contemporary life is present to an untrained eye—her photographs of children, particularly—Greenburg is careful to include a date in the title, as if to make sure we know the photograph is contemporary.

Greenburg began photographing the rockabillies around the time that George W. Bush took office in 2001, and there is a profoundly idealistic, almost irresistibly romantic quality to the rockabillies' lifestyle that appeals deeply to us as the United States emerges from the "War on Terror" and the "assault on reason and science." The series evolved as the photographer herself explored the rockabilly culture and examined her own place within it. There is a rush of infatuation and a measure of melancholy to the earliest works, a sense of yearning that has since waned: "I don't always look longingly at my subjects the way I used to now that the political climate has changed," says Greenburg.[17]

Through Greenburg's eyes, we share in her mixed perspective. Rockabilly is escapism, but it is not the popcorn-and-movie-in-an-air-conditioned-theater kind that most of us seek out; it is unrelenting, exacting, and permanent. The rockabilly life is also an enormously creative and life-affirming way to exist. Greenburg has taken us inside the enigmatic world of the rockabilly subculture, captured it for us, and encouraged us to look beyond its glamorous surface into the compelling substance within.

1   Malcolm Barnard, *Fashion as Communication,* 2nd ed. (London: Routledge, 2002).

2   E-mail message from Jennifer Greenburg to the author, July 29, 2009.

3   Jennifer Greenburg, artist's statement, Hyde Park Art Center http://www.hydeparkart.org/alist/profile/greenburg_jennifer/ accessed July 2009.

4   Craig Morrison, *Go Cat Go!: Rockabilly Music and Its Makers* (Urbana and Chicago: University of Illinois Press, 1996), 15. Morrison cites Steve Tucker, "Rockabilly," an unpublished essay and notes for proposed reissue set of rockabilly recordings (1983), 3.

5   E-mail message from Jennifer Greenburg to author, July 29, 2009.

6   Anne Hollander, *Sex and Suits* (New York: Alfred A. Knopf, 1994), 11.

7   Virginia Postrel, "A Golden World," in *Glamour: Fashion + Industrial Design + Architecture,* ed. Joseph Rosa, et. al. (New Haven: San Francisco Museum of Modern Art in association with Yale University Press, 2004), 24.

8   Penny Sparke, *As Long as It's Pink: The Sexual Politics of Taste* (San Francisco: Pandora, 1995), 172.

9   Simon Doonan, *Wacky Chicks: Life Lessons from Fearlessly Inappropriate and Fabulously Eccentric Women* (New York: Simon & Schuster, 2003), 110.

10   Greenburg, artist's statement.

11   Greenburg, artist's statement, Photo-Eye Gallery http://www.photoeye.com/gallery/forms2/ statement.cfm?id=192480, accessed July 2009.

12   Susan Sontag, *On Photography* (New York: Farrar, Straus & Giroux, 1977), 37.

13   Telephone interview between Jennifer Greenburg and the author, July 31, 2009.

14   Ibid.

15   Roland Barthes, *Camera Lucida,* trans. Richard Howard (New York: Farrar, Straus & Giroux, 1981), 27.

16   Hal Foster, *The Return of the Real* (Cambridge: MIT Press, 1996), 134.

17   E-mail message from Jennifer Greenburg to the author, July 29, 2009.

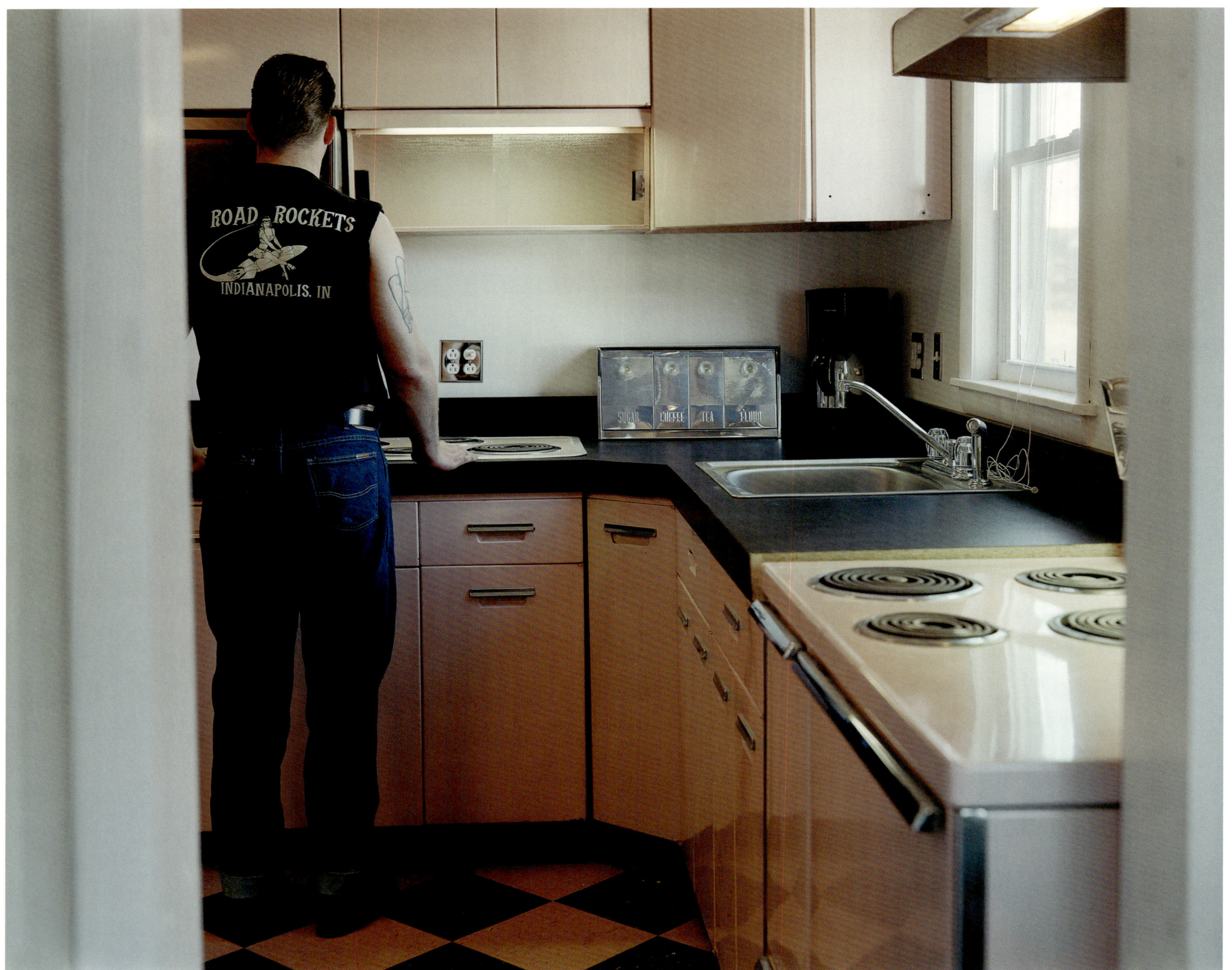
ROAD ROCKETS
INDIANAPOLIS. IN
SUGAR
COFFEE
TEA
FLOUR

Afterword

by Bruce Berenson

When I was a kid growing up in Queens, New York, no one I knew dressed like the people in Jennifer Greenburg's photographs (although I have a picture of myself, age five, in the same outfit as the boy in "Arty the Cowboy" on page 23). Having been born in 1954, just a few months after Elvis Presley stepped into Sun Studios in Memphis to record the sonic explosion of "That's All Right," I remember the pre-Beatle-era rocker look. It tended towards either sharp, shiny imported suits or visual copies of cast members from *West Side Story*. Elvis's "Hillbilly Cat" model just didn't travel well in those days. When the music scene in my hometown diversified in the mid-1970s and disco became nationally ubiquitous, one could easily ignore it in the punk and new wave clubs of Manhattan and the outer boroughs or in the wilds of Long Island, where the kids tended to prefer the Allman Brothers, Marshall Tucker, and the other "jam" bands of the day. I was firmly entrenched in the punk camp, and, happily, it coexisted quite nicely with the first Rockabilly revival here in the States (after having steadily evolved in the United Kingdom and other parts of Europe). I discovered the joys of wearing a pink suit jacket and black tuxedo pants for going out to the Mudd Club (never before midnight, of course), Hurrah's, or CBGBs, where not only could you listen to new bands playing old music, but also be part of a cultural community which selectively combined elements from the past, present, and an anticipated future.

It seems to be our nature as a society to look back at past cultural epochs as a series of snapshots—flashes of remembered or imagined impressions—caricatures of what was a more complex reality. In Greenburg's photographs, you find people who choose to adopt the sartorial and lifestyle trappings of a time period spanning approximately ten years. It is a period now thought to represent conformity and allegiance to a mythologically homogeneous culture as represented by tightly controlled media outlets of the day—luridly portraying rock and roll "rebels" as a threat to our "way of life." Despite the fact that black and white music had been cross-pollinating wherever the races happened to exist in close proximity, this was not generally considered to be a good thing. In the Jim Crow South, where rhythm and blues fused with country and western to make that particularly joyous sound we call Rockabilly, racism was a brutal fact of life that could rear up and strike a person of color for presuming themselves the equal of their white neighbors. Now we look at these images with an affectionate and amused tolerance that would have baffled the original observers. Thank God! It's certainly true that the rebellion against the status quo that the music represented has evaporated over time, and what we now see in the portraits is as collective resistance to mainstream style and what today passes for pop culture. One evening spent surfing the 500 or so channels available on your average cable system could very well drive any thinking person into a simpler past, a monastic existence, or maybe merciful oblivion, but for the Rockabillies it has brought them an alternate reality.

It's important to note that, by and large, the original performers of rock and roll music were not looking for "rebel" status. They wanted what everybody else wanted—the good life as shown on TV, in movies, and in magazine advertisements. Of course, they were musical innovators, but the first thing most of them did with their first royalty check (if they achieved even a modicum of success) was to go out and buy something showy and grand, usually a Cadillac (then a defining symbol of the American Dream). Those who persevered in the music business generally made the shift toward the more conservative (and hence safer) country and western side of the equation.

A particularly interesting anomaly is what the Rockabillies believe to be proper interaction with the mainstream. In the United Kingdom, for example, the look as cultivated by the fans of the rock and roll, known as Teddy Boys, has long been inseparable from a particularly violent culture of hooliganism. France also had Ted equivalents. One can only gape open-mouthed at photos of musical icons, such as Wanda Jackson, Billy Lee Riley, and other Rockabilly survivors, playing in front of appropriately period-dressed crowds of fans in places like Spain, Italy, and Finland (Finland?). Before the Internet, it would have been very difficult to find the appropriate garb. Not only are many of the clothes now made far from the shores of the U. S. A., but the Internet has made it possible for anyone anywhere to order a head-to-toe duplication of the Look. So much for diversity.

Jennifer Greenburg's photographs do what any successful portrait should: make me want to know more about the subjects and, lacking facts, make me want to construct my own life story for them. I wonder what these Rockabillies do for a living and if their worldview is reflected in their aesthetic. Do they always dress like this (even to cousin Marilyn's wedding or Max's bar mitzvah)? Do their musical preferences include The Strokes, Vivaldi, or even Hannah Montana? As unlikely as it is that you would find me holding court in a Hawaiian shirt at my home's basement Tiki bar, or once again hauling out the pink coat and black slacks for an all-nighter, I think there's an honesty and innocence in Jennifer Greenburg's images that demands your attention.

Notes on the Plates

Acknowledgments

WHEN I EMBARKED ON THIS PROJECT NEARLY TEN YEARS AGO, I had no idea that my methods would cost me blood, sweat, tears, and heartache. The shining light at the end of the tunnel came in the form of David and Patricia Schulte. The Schultes embraced me and my artistic vision wholeheartedly, and they launched this project into orbit. Their support and confidence in this project and in my work is unparalleled. Without them, this book would not exist, and I am forever indebted and grateful.

I wish to thank all the rockabillies for being my friends and muses. You are inspirational, exciting, and lovely, and this book is ultimately a tribute to you. Specifically, I wish to thank Jolie Tomasello, Catherine Mayotte, Ilise Carter, Vanessa Little, and Michael Weiss, for serving as my friends and faithful liaisons in unfamiliar cities and for allowing my work to take shape.

Producing a book is so much collaboration between author and editor. The connection between the two is essential. The day I received a message from my editor at the Center for American Places at Columbia College, Brandy Savarese, I knew it was fate that brought her to my project. Brandy's unbridled enthusiasm, quick thinking, and spirit made this book what it is. Without her drive and determination, I, and the project, would have been utterly lost.

When the idea of finding contributors to write about this project arose, I knew that the project must have an essay from the incomparable living lexicon of rockabilly, Bruce Berenson, of Sirius/XM Radio's *The Rockabilly Road Trip*. Bruce's humor and wit combined with his seemingly endless knowledge have provided a very important part of this book. I extend a heartfelt thank you to Audrey Michelle Mast, for writing the perfect critical essay and for the gift of her time. Her attention to detail matched with her critical thinking tied up loose ends. Audrey, your spirit shines above all.

I am grateful for the good taste and personal style of George F. Thompson, the Center's founder and director. His cowboy boots and bolo ties made me certain that he would like my work and accept my pitch! It was kismet. I am also thankful for the vision and wonderful feedback of Justin Kimball, who was my professional reader on this project and who advised and connected me with several opportunities in the art world.

This project is partially supported by a Community Arts Assistance Program grant from the City of Chicago Department of Cultural Affairs and the Illinois Arts Council, a State Agency. I would like to especially thank Lindsey Delahanty, for her enthusiasm toward my work. I would like to thank Jeff Hoone and Hannah Frieser of The Light Work Artist-In-Residency Program for providing me with a wonderful experience in Syracuse and for their continued support.

The production of this book was a complicated and lengthy process. Special thanks are due to Caitlin Arnold, Nathan Baker, and Aron Gent at Blackpoint Editions, for their wonderful drum scans of my negatives. I also thank Jason Stauter, the Center's operations and production manager, for staying cool as a cucumber during my panics and last-minute requests. He is the best of all rocks.

There are so many people in the professional art world to whom I would love to give thanks, but I cannot list them all. A special thanks to Allison Peters-Quinn and the curators at the Hyde Park Art Center, Ann Fritz at the Indiana University Northwest Gallery for Contemporary Art, Lynn Vandenesse and Skip Stockdon at the Richmond Public Library, Melanie McWhorter and the staff at photo-eye in Santa Fe, Darren Ching of *PDN* magazine, Steve Zeifman of Box Set Gallery, Crista Dix of Wallspace Seattle, the Contemporary Art Museum St. Louis, and Karen Irvine, Natasha Egan, and staff of the Museum of Contemporary Photography in Chicago.

The teachers of my past shaped me into the photographer and person I am today, and I give thanks to each and every educator with whom I have been lucky enough to work. I expressly thank Bill O'Donnell, for being my teacher, friend, and colleague for the past fifteen years. Thank you to my esteemed colleagues, Judy Natal and Lynn Sloan at Columbia College Chicago, for nurturing me, befriending me, and advising me during the early stages of this project.

I thank my mother and father, for providing me with the best possible education and for supporting my artistic talents. I am so lucky to have parents who continue to be unruffled through all my insane endeavors—such as driving all night to Minnesota to capture *Mr. Mysterious and Mamie* on page 15, or driving home in a blinding snowstorm after photographing *Tom Culbertson in anticipation of Naomi* on page 5, or missing a family vacation to attend to Viva Las Vegas or the Rockabilly Rebel Weekender in, "of all places, Indianapolis." I hope that the "whirlwind that is Jennifer Greenburg" will keep the two of you forever young. And to my dad, who is most likely the true inspiration for this project, I wish to say thanks for letting me inherit your legacy. I know that I have often cramped your style—spitting up on your suede jackets as an infant, wearing black lipstick and a tutu to my prom, having an ever-rotating group of "strange friends," and wearing those "old lady dresses," but never for one moment have I doubted your faith and love for me, and I consider myself one of the luckiest people on Earth to be your daughter.

And to my perfect husband, Casey, who will never know just how perfect he is, I thank you for always standing beside me and for truly having my best interest at heart at all times. Casey, you are the best friend and partner anyone could ever ask for.

About the Photographer

JENNIFER GREENBURG was born in 1977 and raised in Chicago, Illinois, where she currently resides. She holds a B.F.A. from The School of the Art Institute in Chicago and a M.F.A. in conceptual art (emphasizing documentary video and photography) from the University of Chicago. Solo exhibitions of her work have been held at the Hyde Park Art Center, Chicago; Indiana University Northwest Gallery for Contemporary Art, Gary; The Richmond Public Library, Richmond, Virginia; The Latin School of Chicago; and ARC Gallery, Chicago. Light Work awarded Greenburg a grant and Artist-in-Residency for 2005, publishing a selection of *The Rockabillies* in its 2006 annual, *Contact Sheet*. Greenburg is a recipient of an Illinois Arts Council Grant and two Community Arts Assistant Program (CAAP) Grants. Her work is part of the permanent collections of Light Work and the Museum of Contemporary Photography. Greenburg has taught at Columbia College Chicago, Loyola University Chicago, Harold Washington College in Chicago, and College of Lake County in Grayslake, Illinois.

About the Essayists

BRUCE BERENSON was born in 1954 and raised in Queens, New York, where he attended Queens College. He has dedicated his life to radio, working in broadcast operations at CBS Radio Network for twenty years, before making the switch to satellite radio operations. When Berenson discovered that XM Radio featured none of his favorite artists in its extensive musical lineup, he pitched the idea for "Rockabilly Roadtrip,"an imaginary car ride around the United States sampling different geographic varieties of the genre. Berenson still lives in his hometown of Queens, with his wife and children, and he hosts the "Roadtrip" when not otherwise occupied by his "real" job, Director of New York Operations for the now-merged SIRIUS XM Radio.

AUDREY MICHELLE MAST was born in Detroit in 1977 and raised in Michigan's "thumb" region. She received a B.A. in critical studies of film and video from Columbia College Chicago and a M.A. in modern art theory, history and criticism from the School of the Art Institute of Chicago. Her writing has appeared in *ArtAsiaPacific, Artkrush, GUP* (Netherlands), *Sculpture, TENbyTEN,* and numerous exhibition catalogs, including *Loaded: Hunting Culture in North America* at the Glass Curtain Gallery, Columbia College Chicago; *Nick and Sheila Pye: A Life of Errors,* and *Yes: New Works by Sandra Bermudez,* both at Kasia Kay Gallery, Chicago, in 2006; and *Mike Andrews and Kaylee Rae Wyant: Built According to an Arrangement of Domestic Functions Which Has Now Reached the Final Stage of an Old Concept* at Roots and Culture Contemporary Art Center, Chicago, in 2008. She currently works as a writer, editor, and curator and is based in Chicago, Illinois.

ABOUT THIS BOOK:

The Rockabillies is the sixteenth volume in the *Center Books on American Places* series, George F. Thompson, series founder and director. The book was brought to publication in an edition of 1,500 hardcover copies with the generous financial assistance of David Schulte and the Friends of the Center for American Places, for which the publisher is most grateful. The text was set in Trade Gothic, and the paper is Gold East matte, 150 gsm weight. The book was professionally printed and bound in Singapore. For more information about the Center for American Places at Columbia College Chicago, please see page 96.

FOR THE CENTER FOR AMERICAN PLACES AT COLUMBIA COLLEGE CHICAGO:

George F. Thompson, Founder and Director

Justin Kimball, Consulting Editor

Brandy Savarese, Editorial Director

Jason Stauter, Marketing and Operations Manager

Erin F. Fearing, Executive Assistant

Amber K. Lautigar and A. Lenore Lautigar, Associate Editors and Publishing Liasons

Purna Makaram, Manuscript Editor

Jehan Abon, Book Designer

David Skolkin, Art Director

The Center for American Places at Columbia College Chicago
600 South Michigan Avenue
Chicago, Illinois 60605-1996, U.S.A.
www.americanplaces.org

Distributed by the University of Chicago Press
www.press.uchicago.edu

17 16 15 14 13 12 11 10 09 1 2 3 4 5

Library of Congress Cataloging-in-Publication Data

Greenburg, Jennifer, 1977-
  The rockabillies / by Jennifer Greenburg ; with essays by Bruce Berenson and Audrey Michelle Mast. --
1st ed.
      p. cm. -- (American places)
  Includes bibliographical references.
  ISBN 978-1-930066-99-1 (alk. paper)
  1. Portrait photography--United States. 2. Popular culture--United States--Pictorial works. 3. Families--
United States--Pictorial works. 4. Rockabilly subculture--Pictorial works. I. Title.
  TR681.F28G738 2009
  779'.2092--dc22
                              2009030215

ISBN 13: 978-1-930066-99-1

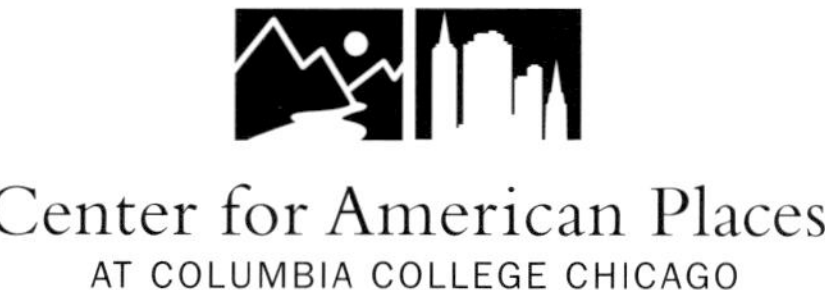